HAUNTS OF THE UPPER GREAT LAKES

Dixie Franklin

Haunts of the Upper Great Lakes ©1997 by Dixie Franklin

Printed in the United States of America

04   5 4 3

ISBN 1-882376-47-1

Cover design by Adventures with Nature

Holt, Michigan

Other titles in the Thunder Bay Press *Tales of the Supernatural* series:
  Haunted Indiana
  Haunted Indiana 2
  School Spirits
  Hoosier Hauntings
  Chicagoland Ghosts
  Floridaland Ghosts
  Michigan Haunts and Hauntings

TABLE OF CONTENTS

Foreword

When the first hint of pale morning light or the taste of the cool of evening creep across Michigan's Upper Peninsula and northern Wisconsin, who can say if the movement in the shadowy forests or the creaking from the old house down the weed-choked path are real? Is the moaning in the trees from the rubbing of their branches? Is it merely a restless breeze that plucks at the kitchen curtain? Do my eyes play tricks on me?

Throughout the years I have pursued stories of people and places and listened with interest to the "other side of the story." At times, the anxious tellers confide their stories to me in a rush of words, as though they can hardly restrain themselves from passing along their eerie tales. Others like the shoe salesman who first told me about the 'Crying Cabin' kept interrupting his story with furtive glances over his shoulder, vowing "never to go back to that place again."

Phil Porter is less sure about the ghost that is said to roam the house where he lives on Mackinac Island. As Chief Curator of Fort Mackinac State Parks, he listens politely. The creaks, groans, and rustlings are said to be that of a lady who lived at Fort Mackinac many years ago. After attending the wake of a man in the house now occupied by the Porters, she was just climbing into a carriage to join the funeral procession when she noticed that her gloves were missing. She hurried back inside to retrieve them. Suddenly, she burst back through the door, eyes wide with terror, gasping that the corpse stowed in the black horse-drawn hearse at the front of the procession was standing inside the door, watching it all. The lady in black is said to forever return, eternally searching for her gloves.

When asked about the ghost, Phil shrugs: "I have five young children at home, so I'm always hearing things that go bump in the night, " he said.

Do I believe in ghosts? I believe in the sincerity of the people who have shared their stories with me. As the gifts of stories have come to me, I have filed them away in a recess of my mind, waiting until they could fill a book. Now I pass them on to you.

Chapter 1
Mystery of the Paulding Light

Dusk creeps slowly along the forested road near Dog Meadow between the sleepy villages of Watersmeet and Paulding in Michigan's Upper Peninsula. After tourists have visited the nearby waterfalls at Bond Falls Flowage and the casino at Watersmeet, they park their cars along Robbins Pond Road in the Ottawa National Forest and gaze down the power line paralleling the old highway that still bears evidence of a long-abandoned railroad grade. They are waiting for the Paulding Light that regularly seems to dance along the wires of the tall power lines.

Then a pinpoint like a firefly appears in the darkness, wavering, growing in brilliance and size, following the wires. The light swings erratically, then disappears. Occasionally smaller red lights appear and fade. All is silent except for the whispers of tourists and wind in the trees.

Though most people refer to the Paulding Light in the singular, the lights do not limit themselves to one occurrence a night, or indeed may not show up at all.

"There almost are as many different theories as there are visitors including that it might be distant headlights from traffic on US-45," said Paul Blettner, Assistant District Ranger, U.S. Forest Service, Watersmeet Ranger Station. He said visitors should be given the option to choose whatever explanation they prefer.

Residents do not recall when the wavering lights were first seen. More than thirty years ago, local teens were thrilling tourists with tales of the light they said followed the lines all the way from Cemetery Road in the distant hills to Dog Meadow. Girls squealed and grabbed their dates in terror. Boys hero-

ically offered protection in their awaiting arms. The best place to hear the stories of the Paulding Light is while standing alongside the road south of Big Rock as twilight slides into full darkness.

Some say the eerie light is the ghost of the pioneer mailman who delivered the mail up and down the old route to Green Bay, Wisconsin. He ran the winter trail by dogsled. One snowy morning when the mail was late, they found him and his dogs, with throats slashed, sprawled beside the sled. The spot where this grisly murder took place is called Dog Meadow to this day. Legend says the lights are those of the murdered mailman, returning night after night to gather up his dogs.

The Forest Service tells a similar tale. A nearby sign reads: PAULDING LIGHT. This is the location from which the famous Paulding Light can be observed. Legend explains its presence as a railroad brakeman's ghost destined to remain forever at the site of his untimely death. He continually waves his signal lantern as a warning to all who come to visit. To observe this phenomenon, park along this forest road facing north. The light will appear each evening in the distance along the power line right-of-way.

Others agree the light is a lantern, but claim the railroad man was the engineer. The story goes that the engineer got into a fight with a lumberjack down at the tavern, defending the honor of his 'shady-lady' love. The lumberjack fought dirty, and the engineer lay dying in the night. Some folks say the railroad man can't rest easy, struck with conscience after losing his life over such a fickle love. He still returns at twilight, searching for his soul.

Other folks lean toward the tale of Pancake Joe. Pancake ran a pool hall in the nearby village of Watersmeet. He saved enough money to buy a rock farm at Paulding along the old Military Road. Life was good for old Pancake until the power lines went through, and he fought it all the way. Folks say he is still fighting, climbing the poles most every night to dance up and down the lines, raising sparks and scaring folks.

"I have noticed that the longer our visitors linger in Jarvi's Bar down in the valley, the brighter the lights seem to be," one long-time resident said.

Visitors who return during the daylight hours see only forest, power lines, and the boulder called Big Rock, where the road curves before ducking down into the valley. One piece of literature gives directions on how to approach the spot where the light appears: "Approximately four miles north of Watersmeet on Highway 45, Robbins Pond Road. Stop at the top of the second hill, park and wait and watch!"

Residents find the light quite comforting. They blame it for everything from uncooperative weather to car problems, cranky spouses, and even an occasional spell of poor fishing.

Chapter 2
Nobody!

With forty-two rooms, three floors, and a full basement and attic, Pine Cottage on Northern Michigan's Mackinac Island has plenty of room for ghosts.

Mackinac Island rises from the waters of Lake Huron a little over three miles off St. Ignace. During the summer months, it bustles with visitors to Fort Mackinac and other historical attractions, fudge and souvenir shops, horse-drawn carriages, and the majestic Grand Hotel. Some days there seems to be more bicycles than people; no motorized vehicles are allowed. There are picnickers in Father Marquette Park; boats joggle for docking space in the marina, and hotels and quaint bed and breakfast inns buzz with guests.

But in the winter, cold winds blow across Mackinac Island. Lake Huron turns to ice and ferries make their last runs. Small commuter planes and snowmobiles are the only transportation across the frozen lake road to the mainland. Until recent years, few tourists ventured to the island from November to late May.

Bob Hughey had come to Mackinac Island as a fifteen-year-old looking for work. He often passed a little shack on the corner of Astor and Market streets. Previously it had been a dry-cleaning shop, now it belonged to a plumber. When Bob was nineteen, the plumber moved out and Bob rented the building, borrowed a few tables, bought some plates, cups and pots, and opened a restaurant

Little Bob's Restaurant did well. Then World War II intervened. His parents moved to the island and ran it while Bob was in the service. Returning home, he married Pat and expanded the restaurant. Business was good.

In the winter of 1962, the Hugheys purchased Pine Cottage. They had never seen the interior of the 1890 structure with a wing to the north and a wraparound front porch but they knew there would be space enough for them and their employees. Bob had closed the purchase of Pine Cottage with the Moral Rearmament people by phone that winter. The group had operated a college and church on the island for several years. Now they were selling their property and moving on.

Pine Cottage sits halfway up Bogan Lane, less than two blocks from Lake Huron. It is a 'walk-your-bicycle'-steep narrow paved lane that ends at the base of East Bluff. Houses are crowded together, with narrow beds of flowers and front steps that lead directly down onto the lane. The house has a wooden glass-paned door leading to an entrance hall. Straight ahead is a staircase. To the right is a small living area and a dining room. Windows throughout the house are tall and narrow.

The Hugheys regularly escaped to Scottsdale, Arizona, for the winter where Bob worked as a chef. When spring came and the ice melted, they returned to Mackinac Island.

Bob Hughey first realized there was 'something there' in Pine Cottage one night in the early spring of 1962. Bob was playing cards with his brother Joe, sister-in-law Becky, and his cook. It was good to be back on the island, even though he missed Pat who had stayed in Scottsdale to allow the five kids to finish out their school year. In a few days, Bob expected that the ferries would be bringing the rest of the restaurant help from St. Ignace and Mackinaw City. But tonight, Bob's mind was on his card game.

The card game was lively, with bantering back and forth as night shadows darkened the windows. His small dog, Chipper, sat at his feet, occasionally slapping her fuzzy tail against the hardwood floor as though to applaud the jovial laughter at the table.

Suddenly, above the chatter, Bob heard the heavy front door open and close, then the echo of footsteps on the stairs. Joe looked up from his cards. "Somebody came in," he said.

"Yeah, I heard them, too," Bob replied. He dropped his cards on the table and went to check. Nobody was there. He called out. Nobody. They searched the house. Nobody!

Then he recalled the stories he had heard from the Moral Rearmament people. During the sale of Pine Cottage to Bob, they had mentioned that the house was haunted. Anxious to close, Bob had paid little heed.

The day after the card game, he explained the strange footsteps to Pat on the phone. With the kids to care for and packing to do, she was more concerned with which bedroom would be hers. "If we're thinking about using the extra space for employees, check out all the bedrooms now. I want the one with the biggest closet," she told him.

Pat has a merry disposition and laughter comes easily. With her contagious smile and hair filled with glints of slow firelight, she brings sunshine to a room. A deeply religious child, she grew up in Goetzville in Michigan's extreme eastern Upper Peninsula, a small village across Lake Huron from Mackinac Island. In 1952 and just out of high school, Pat had come to Mackinac Island where she found work at the Lakeview Hotel. Then she met Bob.

After his call to Arizona, Bob climbed the stairs to choose a room for Pat. Chipper was at his heels. On the first floor at Room 4, he opened the door. Suddenly he froze. A woman burst from a closet and rushed madly toward him. But only half a woman! Her hair was in a bun and her eyes were riveting glowing red. But he could only see her from the waist up. On she rushed. She bumped into him, almost knocking him over, and flew right out the window!

"Little Chipper barreled out of there. She would never go back into that room," Bob recalls.

But that was just the beginning. Pat recalls that over the years, there seemed to always be something going on. "More so in the fall of the year," she says. "But we were not afraid of the ghosts." Pat had been legally blind for years, with only limited vision. "So I never saw anything," she says with good-natured laughter. "But I often sensed something was there.

Sometimes when I was upstairs soaking in a bath, I would feel somebody watching me. I felt the presence. I often turned to look behind me. If anything was there, I couldn't see it."

At other times, Chipper seemed to see things the others could not. Home alone one evening, Pat saw Chipper suddenly leap off the bed as though startled. She darted across to the middle of the room and jumped up as though to greet a friend. Nobody was there.

Pat said Bob was more apprehensive than the rest of the family, especially after seeing the woman with the red eyes. Employees tended to be frightened of the ghosts. Pat's mother didn't like them at all.

When the Hughey's five children were small, Pat's mother and father moved to the island during the busy summer months to help care for them while their parents worked in the restaurant. One morning, young Darwin asked, "Grandma, what were you doing standing by my bed last night?"

"Honey, I wasn't in your room last night," she replied.

"Yes, you were, Grandma. And you had on a long dress," Darwin insisted.

She turned the question away lest she frighten him. "I came to cover you up," she said. Later she related the story to Pat. "But I was not in his room," she insisted to her daughter.

Unexplained sightings have continued over the years. After the Hugheys converted Pine Cottage to a tourist home, Pat said her mother refused to go upstairs. "She would hand the guests the keys to their room, and let them find their own way," Pat laughed.

Tourists sometimes commented on a 'big white thing' moving across their window or a cold space in their room on the warmest of nights. Children complained that someone tried to push them from their beds.

The Hughey's son Dwaine and his wife, Cindy, converted the third floor into an apartment. Their two-year-old regularly complained that 'somebody is pushing me out of bed.' Cindy grew accustomed to hearing something, or someone, rummaging in her child's toy box when the rest of the house was quiet.

"I put crosses in all the rooms and statues all around," Pat says. "I brought in statues from both Catholic churches. There was nothing else I could do."

Pat said a lot of sightings have centered around a little girl with long straight blonde hair and big eyes filled with tears. Once, after the eleven a.m. check-out time, her daughter Yvonne was getting dressed for work at the restaurant. Hearing a child screaming outside her bedroom, she rushed to open the door to find a little girl sobbing in the hall. She saw Yvonne and turned to run. She darted around the corner with Yvonne in pursuit. However, when Yvonne reached the corner, she stopped abruptly. The hall was empty. The little girl was gone.

The wispy child seemed to be everywhere. Late one evening Cindy encountered her in the kitchen of the big house. The little girl was just standing there. As Cindy moved toward her, the child dashed toward the wall and disappeared.

Pat said nobody heard a sound from the child except the crying until a cook from the restaurant spoke to her. The Hugheys had converted Pine Cottage to a tourist home and moved the employee housing across Bogan Lane to what is now Chateau Lorraine Bed & Breakfast. The tourist season was over. The air was crisp and the last of the autumn leaves carpeted the ground with red and gold. One of the cooks had stayed behind to help Bob close the restaurant for the winter, and was still living in employee housing.

Pat said the trembling cook came to them. He told how he had stepped from the bathroom into the hallway with only a towel wrapped around his waist. "He said a little girl was standing there, crying. He asked her what the matter was, and she said, `Mommie, I want to come home'. He reached out to comfort her, and she disappeared."

The cook quit the next day, never to return.

One day a stranger knocked at the Hughey's door to inquire if they were aware that their little girl was in the attic. Bob thanked the man, but explained that the attic was locked.

"But I saw her there. She was standing in the window crying," the stranger said.

Finally, Pat asked a neighbor if anything had ever happened to a little girl who might have lived at Pine Cottage. "She told me that many years ago there had been a little girl who had lived there during the summers. Her parents drank heavily and left the girl alone a lot. After they moved back to Detroit I heard that the little girl had died," Pat explained.

Pat said the sightings were not limited to the little girl; others involved houses and people up and down Bogan Lane. One resident sent her children off to school, then returned to do her household chores. She was picking up clothes in a bedroom when she glanced at a mirror. She saw the reflection of a man looking back at her. Startled, she turned. There was nobody else in the room.

Late one winter day, when the Hugheys were staying year-round on Mackinac Island, Bob looked out the window of Pine Cottage and saw in the window of the closed-up house next door the shape of a man silhouetted against the glass, arms outstretched 'as though pasted against the panes.' Bob rushed outside. From below, he could not see the figure. There were no tracks in the snow leading to the house. Back inside his own home, he looked again at the window. The man was gone.

That winter the Hugheys closed off the heat on the second and third floors and moved into the downstairs. "One night, Bob and I had a quarrel. He huffed out to sleep upstairs in our cold summer room," Pat said. "I thought, well, I'll have the room to myself for a few days."

During the night Bob came back down, scared stiff. "Can I sleep with you?" he asked meekly.

"Why?" Pat laughed. "Is something after you?" Bob didn't answer, but crawled into the bed beside her.

The next morning he told her that he had woken in the night because someone was pulling at his covers. He tugged back but the somone, or something, pulled at them again. Soon it was a tug of war. Finally, he opened his eyes and in the moonlight, he saw something like a man on his hands and knees beside the bed. He had what appeared to be horns growing out of his back. He ran for Pat's bed.

Their son Kevin also had an encounter with a ghost. After working the night shift at the restaurant, he returned home about 11:30 p.m. He was fumbling with the keys to his room when, without a sound, something like a wheelchair struck hard against the back of his legs. He spun around to an empty hall. Kevin slept downstairs for several nights.

The ghosts moved with the Hugheys. In 1976, they built an addition onto Little Bob's Restaurant, with living quarters upstairs and Pat's gift shop next door. Bob and Pat had bedrooms across the hall from each other; the rest of the building was employee housing. One night after the restaurant had been closed and locked, Pat heard the door to the stairs open and footsteps come down the hall. Then the footsteps stopped.

Pat called out, "Bob, was that you who just came in and slammed the door?"

"No," he yelled from across the hall. "I'm in the bathtub. But somebody came in. I heard it, too."

Nobody was there.

Pat said she grew accustomed to the footsteps. She heard them regularly walking back and forth upstairs above the gift shop. But, the ghosts haven't been around since Pat's father died at their home in Goetzville in 1983. After the funeral, Bob decided he would stay a few more days. Deer season was opening soon. He would keep Pat's mother company and hunt a little. "Since we were leaving in two weeks for Arizona, we decided Mother could keep our dogs. She needed the company," he said.

Pat and her daughter Yvonne returned to the island. That night as Pat prayed for her departed father, she recalls, "I was praying hard. The only other sound was the record player on low. Then I heard a voice in the room swearing. It was a nasty masculine voice, a hoarse whisper. I was startled, but I prayed harder than ever until I fell asleep."

She awoke again at five the next morning. It was dark and cold. "I didn't want to get up. I thought I'd lay there until dawn and I prayed some more. Then I heard a gruff snort like a bull."

But eventually Pat decided it was time to rise. Finding Yvonne sleeping downstairs, Pat inquired about her night. "Something was on my bed, panting like a dog," Yvonne replied. Pat reminded her that both their dogs were in Goetzville. "I know," Yvonne said.

Islanders don't attempt to explain their ghosts. Some see them. Some don't. Trish Martin of Bogan Lane Inn says every abandoned house on Mackinac Island has its ghost story, but she has never encountered one. Pat Hughey says ghosts on Mackinac Island come as no surprise to her. After all, Mackinac Island was a gathering place for Native Americans and has been ruled by the French, British, and the Americans. Battles have been fought and great treaties negotiated there. It has been the home of voyageurs and fur traders, the rich and famous, the gentle and the violent, soldiers, priests, industrialists, carriage drivers, and young teens looking for summer jobs in the fudge shops to pay next semester's college tuition.

One rainy night in 1942, a woman who lived in Pine Cottage was murdered. Someone claimed to have seen a figure dressed as a handyman coming down the hill pushing a two-wheel cart the islanders use to transport luggage. Others recall the sounds of horses' hooves and the metal-rimmed wheels of a light carriage being whipped up Turkey Hill toward Fort Mackinac. The murder was never solved.

In 1995, the Hugheys moved to St. Ignace, Michigan and opened a new restaurant, the Last Frontier. It has a western decor, with waitresses in jeans and six-shooters slung at their waists. So far, the ghosts haven't followed them.

And on Mackinac Island, the new owners of Pine Cottage are waiting for the ghosts to come calling.

Chapter 3
Manhattan, With Two Cherries

Old buildings talk in the dark nights of the north country. Boards creak and stairs groan. Lingering flames in the fireplace snap and pop. Outside a tree branch rubs against the house and the wind pops a shingle high on the roof. Who can answer to all the sounds of the night?

Some say ghosts and spirits show a preference for guest houses and inns along the Great Lakes, moving from room to room, walking the halls, restlessly reviewing their memories of times past.

"I don't fault them for coming back," says Joan Jesse, owner of the Wolf River Lodge near Langlade in the heart of Wisconsin's river country. "I love this lodge so much that when I leave I plan to return in whatever form I can find."

The hemlock log walls of Wolf River Lodge blend nicely into the tall pines on a terraced ridge along the wild and scenic Wolf River. Inside, past the dining room with its mismatched chairs and bright red table coverings, is a cozy den crowded with the past. Overstuffed couches stand at right angles to a great stone fireplace, themselves flanked by tables stacked with heavy scrapbooks, glass cases of mementos, and historical pictures lining the walls. As the fire crackles merrily, it is easy to see faces in the flames. Upstairs, subtle sounds make one turn uneasily: a rustle, a creaking of the timbers, the stirring of a curtain.

Joan says hers is a helpful ghost who assists in keeping the lodge running smoothly. "If we need summer rains, it rains here first," she says. "During the winter if we need snow, it snows here when it is not snowing anyplace else."

No sightings have been reported, but unexplainable things have happened that Joan and the maids find comforting—a coverlet straightened, towels replaced, pillows fluffed—things that help make guests feel welcome. Joan feels the presence is that of Helen Steed who, with her husband George, owned the lodge from 1971 to 1988.

"She is the best kind of ghost," Joan said.

———

Mischievous is what employees at Stout Lodge call their ghosts on the small wooded twenty-six-acre island in Red Cedar Lake near the northern town of Mikana, Wisconsin . . . except for the presence that inhabits the bowling alley or occasionally rings the big dinner bell that tops the tall stone column at the lodge's front door.

The summer lodge stands on a bank above the boat house on the Isle of Happy Days and was first built of unpeeled and untreated native white pine in 1903 by Frank Stout. It was tall timber that brought Henry Stout, Frank's father, to the area in the 1870s. Following a big storm in 1875, Stout and his partner in the Knapp, Stout & Company moved to Red Cedar Lake to harvest a big windfall of timber. The operation took off and soon they had fifty-five logging camps scattered around the area. Lumberjacks harvested 85,000 acres of timber and floated the logs down the Cedar River to market.

By 1900, all the tall timber was gone. Sons Frank and Harry inherited their father's fortune. Harry went on to found Stout University, now the University of Wisconsin-Stout at Menomonie. Frank moved to Chicago where he became a director of the Chicago, St. Paul and Omaha Railroad.

But Frank loved the north woods. He owned Rice Lake and the two small islands in its northern end. On the larger island, he built a log lodge as a summer home. No expense was spared. The main lodge was designed after the Adirondack camps of the east. A wide entrance hall separated the beamed dining room and Great Room. Ornately carved beams were imported from Germany. Fireplaces of native stones, solid and sturdy, dominated the rooms. The planked floors were four inches thick. A wing was built to accommodate guests, with porches and rooms with their own wood-burning fireplaces. Each of the Stout children had their own cottage, named in their honor, on the island. The Stouts spent their summers swimming from the dock and raft, playing tennis on the clay court, entertaining in the large recreation hall with its own bowling lane, and golfing at the Tagalong Golf Course on the mainland.

In 1912, Frank noticed that all was not well on his Isle of Happy Days. Insects had burrowed into the bark and eaten away at the square logs of the lodge. Frank ordered a trainload of cedar logs from Idaho, tore down the original lodge, and rebuilt it of cedar. The total cost was 1.5 million dollars.

For the next few years, all was well until Frank developed heart problems. *My ticker's getting bad*, he thought as he brooded about his island getaway from his office in Chicago. Finally, when he felt his time was near he expressed his wish to die on his island and he boarded a plane to fly north. Sadly, he died of a heart attack at Rice Lake, just twenty miles from his Isle of Happy Days.

It is said that Mrs. Stout 'freaked out' after Frank's death. Although she lived for many more years, she was plagued by hallucinations and senility. One day she was found standing on a terrace above the lake with a box of china at her feet. One by one, she picked up each dish and heaved it out into the lake as far as she could sail it.

Over the years, the lodge has become a tourist and corporate getaway, as well as a romantic setting for weddings which are held on the wide sloping terrace lined with well-kept flower beds. From the mainland, beginning in May and continuing through the end of October, visitors arrive by ferry. Upon their arrival, they climb the winding steps from the boat house to a weathered gray lodge that shows its age in subtle ways that betray its past.

Inside the lodge, historical photos line the Great Room. You can curl up in one of the oversized chairs in front of a warm fire to scan a scrapbook from a nearby shelf. The spacious master bedroom and other guest rooms have their own wood-burning fireplaces—fifteen in all. Much of the furnishings are originals, with four-poster beds and aging mirrors hanging over wooden bureaus. Standing at a second-floor bedroom window and gazing across the roof and eaves choked with last year's fallen leaves, it is easy to imagine the stories told about the island.

And there are stories. "The lodge has three haunted areas—Rooms 3 and 5, and the bowling alley," said one employee. "We call our ghost Mary. In the hallway between Rooms 3 and 5, Mary plays with me all the time."

One spring before the first guests arrived, the manager discovered that the lights were on in Room 3. He turned them off and returned to his apartment. The next time he looked, the lights were on again. Three times he retraced his steps to turn off lights. On his last trip, just short of the door he heard the sound of the switch as the light was turned off. "Good, leave them that way," he said aloud. And she does.

One manager said every time he replaces a light bulb, he scolds, "Mary, please leave it alone!" And she does.

Some workers became accustomed to the unexplained happenings, but one maid was very startled when new logs in the cold fireplace of Room 5 suddenly flamed bright red on their own.

Happenings in the bowling alley and recreation center are more visible. A few years ago, a director was setting up for a play that was to be performed in the recreation center. He was alone. Suddenly a crash reverberated through the building, followed by stumbling, shuffling sounds. With the hairs on his neck standing on end, he left the building and refused to return until accompanied by a lodge employee.

Still stranger is the shadowy figure of a man who keeps showing up in pictures taken in the bowling alley and recreation hall. One guest, who insisted there was no ghost, took his video camera, set it up in the bowling alley and waited. When he heard a noise he clicked on the camera. The view finder was blank. No indicator lights clicked on. The camera was dead.

He took the camera outside and checked the view finder again. It worked just fine—there was the pagoda on the lawn and the lake beyond. Mystified, he returned to the bowling alley and again set up the camera. Something scraped across the floor. He quickly peered through the lens. Blank again!

Is the shadowy figure on film Frank's brother Harry? Or Frank himself, trying to make it home?

———

In the village of Big Bay, north of Marquette in Michigan's Upper Peninsula, Darrell Small thought his Thunder Bay Inn had a ghost until he discovered an electrical problem. Lights switched on and off, seemingly without human help, and radios blared suddenly in the middle of the night.

Thunder Bay Inn is steeped in the past. In 1940, Henry Ford remodeled an old company general store into a hotel for his corporate executives near his Huron Mountain retreat. Later it became a movie set for Otto Preminger's *Anatomy of a Murder*. Darrell and his wife Eileen have remodeled and restored it to a country inn of the 1920s era.

Ghosts could certainly feel comfortable in the Great Room furnished with white wicker or in the upstairs hallways. But Darrell says the ghosts are less bothersome since he upgraded the electrical system.

However, no waitress or housekeeper will linger long in the dark. "I am always anxious for daylight and people when I'm rushing up those basement stairs," one confessed.

———

At nearby Big Bay Point Lighthouse Bed and Breakfast, numerous guests have confessed to hearing footsteps walking on the wooden floors at all hours. "Sometimes he turns off lights or opens and closes doors. Two guests claim to have seen him," says owner Linda Gamble. She believes the ghost is the lighthouse's first keeper, William Pryor, who hanged himself in 1904 in the nearby woods.

The red brick lighthouse was built in 1896 on a sandstone cliff overlooking Lake Superior. It houses two apartments built around a square light tower topped by a white steel watch tower. One apartment was for the keeper and the other for the keeper's assistant. Linda now welcomes guests to seven rooms and two suites. Guests enjoy sunsets from the tower and breakfast.

One evening, a guest was preparing for bed in her upstairs room. As she glanced into the bathroom mirror, she saw the reflection of a tall man wearing a keeper's hat behind her. Startled, she whirled around. The room was empty.

Another female guest staying in the same room, awoke in the night to see a figure standing at the end of her bed. She said it was that of a man, in clothing similar to that of a lighthouse keeper. The room was located on the side of the house where Pryor had lived.

───

In Wisconsin's north country near the village of Winter, Tom and Susan Mike are working hard to restore the charm of Barker Lake Country Lodge. The old-fashioned two-story lodge was built in the 1920s by Joe Saltis, a gangster from southwestern Chicago. A summer place in the lake country was a favorite past time for gangsters. Al "Scarface" Capone had The Hideout several miles farther north. In fact, Capone was one of the first guests when Saltis opened the lodge and golf resort.

Saltis, called 'Polack Joe,' started out as a saloonkeeper in Joliet, Illinois. He paid allegiance to Capone while secretly joining up with gangster Earl 'Hymie' Weiss. Soon he moved into Chicago and headed up the Saltis-McEarlene gang which controlled the illegal liquor distribution on Chicago's south side. Newspapers of the era noted that anybody who crossed Saltis went out feet-first.

Up north, Saltis entertained at his cream-colored country lodge beside Barker Lake and bought drinks for his friends with hundred-dollar bills. Down south, police issued a nationwide all-points bulletin to bring him in. Metro papers picked up the news and pasted it on their front pages.

Meanwhile, Saltis was engaging in his favorite sport of fly fishing. Unaccustomed to following rules, he ventured beyond the warning sign and got caught fishing in a prohibited area

five hundred feet below a state-owned dam. Volunteer deputies led by a game warden swarmed in, captured Saltis and his whole gang, and hauled them before the local magistrate. Unaware of national headlines or the all-points bulletin, the magistrate dutifully assessed the maximum fines and let them go.

Later Saltis put up his resort as a bet to a buddy in a card game, and lost it. He died penniless in a Chicago flophouse.

His association with the lodge is felt in the wide sweep of grass down to the lake, along the hallway lined with guest rooms, and on the popular nine-hole golf course winding through the tall pines for which he had brought in truckloads of top soil from Tennessee.

Nevertheless, Saltis does not seem to haunt the resort. Rather, the ghost may be that of a former owner. Harry Mueller operated the lodge until four years before Tom and Susan Mike bought it. Mueller retired and moved to Florida. He bought a house off a golf course fairway, but soon tired of watching others playing golf. He found he missed the green sloping hills of Wisconsin and to satisfy his yearnings, he built berms along his property line and seeded them with grass. Neighbors complained and an argument ensued over his mini-hills. In the heat of the conflict, Harry suffered a heart attack and died.

The Mikes moved to the lodge in early spring and found much work ahead of them. As they began to move things around and position them for the early May opening, they noticed that the furniture would be re-shifted, a bed would be rumpled as though slept in or towels would be hung awry. "One of the former owners must not like the way we're doing things," they joked.

One rainy evening, Tom and the chef were scrubbing the kitchen areas of the lodge. They mopped their way through the building to the front door where they propped up the mop, turned off the lights, and locked up.

"Let's run into town for a beer," Tom said.

Two hours later, as they made the wide swing around the end of the golf course, they noticed the lights were on in the bar. Tom stopped at the cabin he and Sue shared, and asked her, "Have you been up to the bar?" She had not.

They returned to the bar to check for burglars. The door was still locked just as they had left it. Cautiously, they turned the key. Inside, the mop still stood beside the door. No tracks of tell-tale mud marred the clean floor. Venturing into the bar, they found it empty. But at the corner of the bar—at Harry's usual stool was a cocktail tub with ice, half-melted as though it had been there for some time. A trace of red still showed at the bottom of the glass and on the bar napkin next to the glass lay two cherry stems.

Tom inquired around. When he asked a longtime employee about Harry's favorite drink, the employee replied, "Always the same. Manhattans, with two cherries. And he always laid the stems on his napkin."

Chapter 4

Married Man

He lowered his half-empty cup of coffee. It rattled against the saucer. The wind stirred in the tall maples outside the window. Somewhere down in the valley, a dog barked.

"I'll tell you a story," he said. "It was about fifteen years ago. I had driven over to Ontonagon for a meeting with one of those groups you find yourself involved in. It was still early when the meeting broke up, so fifteen or twenty of the guys stopped off at a little bar on Military Road for coffee or a drink.

"The bartender—she's the reason for my story—was a cute little thing. Blonde, with a very pleasant face. She had all the curves that make guys look more than once. She came up from Texas to work for the summer. I think she was related to the bar owners.

"I noticed her, but not really. She was just someone pouring coffee and bringing over the rounds of drinks. This was fifteen years ago and I was a married man, you see. The talk at the table was on the business of the day. It was early so we had the bar to ourselves."

He stopped as though mentally picturing the bar and the crowd. He was soft-spoken and chose his words carefully, mulling them over in his mind. Reaching for his cup again, he lifted it, then idly set it down again without taking a drink.

"Eventually it got on toward dark. Then the door opened and three rough-looking guys pushed their way in. They pulled their stools up to the bar and ordered. There was loud talk between them. After awhile some of our guys reached for their wallets to pay up, getting ready to head home. Suddenly, the girl was there behind me, polite but anxious. I don't know why she picked me. I hadn't given her any time, just ordered coffee and talked with the guys. But she asked me real quiet-like if I was in a hurry. There was an urgency in her voice as she said quietly that she was uneasy about being left alone with the three loud characters at the bar. She said they were strangers around there. She asked if I could stick around until the relief bartender came on. Remember, I was a married man. But something in her voice or the anxiety in her eyes made me want to stay.

"Halfway through my next cup of coffee, her shift changed and she could leave. She thanked me. The three drunks were getting louder, so I walked her to her car.

"Shadows were already deep over Military Road. From the conversation she had picked up around the bar, she feared they might try to follow her. She asked if I would go with her for one drink at a bar down the road. It wasn't far, you know. No more than a few miles. I was beginning to wonder about her. But she seemed so frightened, so I said I could do that.

"The guys didn't show up. She—I can't recall her name— she told me about her decision to move up from Texas. There was a child. Seems like she said it was a little girl.

"At Ontonagon, she said, she had shared a cabin in the foothills of the Porcupine Mountains with another woman. Life was getting better until just a week ago. Then suddenly, in the middle of the night, she heard someone screaming. It came from her roommate's room. She rushed in and switched on the light. The roommate was twisting and turning in her bed as though trying to push something or someone away, her hands clutching at her throat. The roommate was screaming, `He's trying to choke me. He's trying to choke me.' Over and over, she called out while she fought something the girl couldn't see. Then with one big push, the roommate fell back on the bed, sobbing. Then she got up and ran for the door.

"The bartender remembered the sand stinging her face and laying rough on her tongue as she stood in the doorway of the cabin with the dark all around her—except for the headlights of her roommate's car as it kicked up the sand and cut a path through the trees. She wasn't scared then, she said, wondering instead if her roommate had been on drugs. She stayed at the cabin, and nothing else happened that night.

"A few nights later—a dark night with no moon—the girl was again awakened by screaming—her own this time. She said she felt hands grab at her and she leapt up screaming. She grabbed the child, who was frightened and screaming, and ran for her car, playing out the same scene she had watched her roommate play a few nights before, tires throwing sand into the open doorway of the cursed cabin.

"Then the girl sat quietly for awhile, occasionally gesturing as though to speak, trembling hands lifting the glass to her lips. Finally, she said she had left all of her clothes in the cabin. And the child's clothes. She said the little girl cried for her toys. But she couldn't go back.

"Now I was a married man with a wife and children," he said. "But somehow I found myself wanting to help this frightened girl or maybe just wanting to see the cabin for myself. But I think it was the girl. So I said I would drive her back there and wait while she gathered up her things.

"She sat in the dim bar looking at me, drumming her fingers against her glass. But she didn't seem to be interested in me, except for someone to listen to her story. Finally she said 'No,' Her uncle had offered to go with her the next day and it would be too hard to go back in the dark. She wanted to go back with daylight all around her and sun bright in the trees.

"I saw her to her old car, then watched as the glow of tail lights disappeared. My road seemed a long way home that night.

"That's the end of my part of the story. You might go back to the bar and ask around, but that was fifteen years ago. I never went back. I was a married man. But sometimes I wish I had."

Chapter 5

There Goes Willie

When chandeliers sway without the hint of a breeze or the faint aroma of bayberry invades an upstairs dining room of the Chippewa Club in Iron Mountain, Michigan, waitresses say, "There goes Willie!" They talk about lights that go on and off, doors that slam, a piano that plays by itself, the haunting sounds of a crying baby, and small catastrophes that could have been far worse.

"It is a certain sense of presence. After a visit to the lower wine cellar, I sometimes find myself taking the stairs two steps at a time," says a waitress.

But sometimes it is more, especially after any renovation to the three-story Victorian home that has served business and professional leaders of the community for many years. The home was built for mining officials in 1898 and became a private dinner club in 1945, providing a fine-dining atmosphere and social meeting place for members and their guests.

Club manager Mike Moreska said he noticed unusual happenings soon after his arrival twenty years ago. "I've always believed in a practical reason for everything, but too many things have happened that are unexplainable to my sense of logic," Mike says.

A tall burly man with a gregarious personality, Mike at first ignored such things until he stayed late one Saturday night to prepare the Monday payroll. It was well after midnight and he was still working in his office on the main level of the restaurant just off the dining room when he heard what sounded like a crying baby. It was coming from the basement used for storage. Thinking a cat had sneaked in the door as the last of his staff had left for the night, he flipped on the lights and made his way downstairs. The crying seemed to be coming from a room that had been used as a barber shop/shower room when the house was owned by the Otto Conrad Davidson family. Later, the room had served as a storage room, then had been cleared out when the space was no longer needed.

Proceeding down the hall, he was at first unruffled, but he grew more apprehensive as the sound grew louder. Approaching the door, he turned the knob, abruptly shoved open the door and switched on the light in one fluid movement. The crying stopped! Before him was empty shelves against stone basement walls. There was no place for even a cat to hide.

Well, that's the end of payroll for tonight, he thought. Mike switched off the light, walked back up the stairs, took care of the rest of the lights, turned the key in the lock and went home. On Monday he announced that there would be no more late night payrolls while he was manager of the Chippewa Club. Payroll would be made out on Monday from that day forward, with payday on Tuesday. "From then on, very seldom would I be in the club alone that late at night," he says.

The white Colonial Revival three-story structure at the north end of Carpenter Avenue was constructed by the Chapin Mining Company for their general manager, James MacNaughton. Below is the city and remnants of the Chapin Mine. The gabled roof is cut with dormers. To the right of the entrance, the formal staircase is backed by the original stained-glass window with light dancing through in tones of amber and red. Finely-carved mantels top the four fireplaces; high oak wainscoting frames the walls.

The city of Iron Mountain was only twenty years old when the fine home was built. James MacNaughton lived in the home only two years before he was transferred to Calumet. The new general manager, O. C. Davidson and wife Charlotte Dickinson Davidson, occupied it from 1901 until it was sold in 1945 to become the Chippewa Club.

Moreska says the Dickinson's son Willie catches the blame, or the credit, for a number of occurrences at the Chippewa

Club. "There are instances that indicate that we have nothing to fear. The presence is probably a good presence," he said.

One morning Mike walked into the Club and immediately detected the odor of hot electrical wiring, a stench that is easily identifiable. He traced it to wires trailing from a large electrical motor that had shorted out, its wires burned back toward the distribution box and main power outlet. His heart raced when he realized what could have happened if the fire had reached the circuit breaker and the wooden walls.

"Although there had been nobody in the building when the fire occurred, the main breaker switch had been pulled. Because of where the power box was located, the switch had to have been shut off manually," Mike notes.

Since then there has been other small fires and minor floods. For whatever reason, there has always been someone who would come into the building at odd, yet important times, to save it. "Yet there is no logical explanation why that person would come in at midnight or four a.m.," Mike says.

Mike has become accustomed to leaving the building after he makes his usual rounds to turn down the heat, empty the ash trays and garbage, and walk from the top to the bottom of the Club shutting off the lights except for the three that are left on. "Then when I'm driving away, I turn back to see a light in the attic, or the basement light go on," he says.

Bartender Mary Formell's first encounter with the presence in the Club was some years ago. The Club was empty, except for two couples sitting around the horseshoe curve at the end of the bar and the dishwasher in the kitchen. The couples were in lively conversation, enjoying their last cocktail of the evening.

"The dishwasher would always wait for me to close up, so I stepped back to tell him I wouldn't be long," she recalled.

As they talked, Mary heard the piano playing in the front parlor. Thinking the club members had stopped in the parlor to say good-night with a bit of a tune, she returned to the bar. The piano was no longer playing, but the two couples were still in casual conversation in the same seats at the bar.

"This is not a player piano. There was no way they could have gone to the parlor, played a tune and returned to the bar in that short a time. I was less than thirty seconds away," she says. Mary went back to the service station where the bartender was idly drinking a cola.

"Ready to go?" he asked.

"They're still here," she said. "Did you hear the piano playing before I went back into the bar?"

"Sure. I thought they were leaving."

A waitress tells of assisting a medical society group prepare for a seminar by helping to set up tables and adjust lighting for the projector. Several members of the group were working around the podium. As she turned to leave, she switched off the lights, thinking it would improve the viewing when the projector was switched on. Immediately, she was aware that her premature actions had left the workers in darkness. Turning, she moved to switch the lights back on. But before she could reach the doorway, the lights suddenly filled the room, illuminating the workers at the front.

Much of the activity seems to center around the ladies first floor restroom. The room has had several functions: first as a mud room, then as a bar, and finally as the ladies room. It is normally toasty warm. However, especially during the holiday party season, the management receives complaints that the room is icy cold. Freezing, it is said, no matter how the thermostat is adjusted.

The room was the Club's bar in the days when an Italian gardener/caretaker was part of the staff. One evening, the caretaker lingered late, chatting with the bartender before the dinner crowd arrived. He complained of the cold. The bartender suggested he go home, but the caretaker said he would first go outside and take down the flag.

Returning to the bar, he sat down on a stool, and again spoke of how cold he was. Unfolding the flag, he wrapped it around his shoulders and sat cocooned in the Stars and Stripes. The bartender left the room for supplies. When he returned, the caretaker was slumped at the bar, dead. So folks wonder if

P. Reed

he comes around from time to time to make sure everything is in order.

But others insist that the presence is that of Willie, the son of Captain William Edmund Dickinson, who had moved to the small community of Commonwealth near the Wisconsin-Michigan border to take over the management of the Commonwealth Iron Mine.

The Dickinson family settled into the home that the mining company had provided for them, just down the road from the schoolhouse. One day after school, Willie stopped at his uncle's house to pick up a black Ulster coat he had left there earlier. The weather was beginning to turn cool; he might need the coat and the red mittens left in a pocket. Telling his aunt that he was in a hurry to get home, he headed off down the road.

A teamster from the mine turned down the road that ran through the dense forest past the superintendent's home, past the road that led to the Frenchman's farm, past the uncle's home and the school. Just beyond the Frenchman's farm, the teamster spotted two men beside the road. At the same moment, the men apparently heard the wagon. They turned and hastily ducked into the woods. The teamster noted their fine clothes. "Sure don't work in the mines," he muttered, but thought no more of it.

Down the road, he spotted Willie. He was a talkative youngster with folks he knew, but shy with strangers. Willie, almost six years old, was large for his age, with easy contagious laughter that spread in a grin across his face and almost squeezed his blue eyes shut. The teamster stopped. "Want a ride, Willie?"

Willie grinned. He loved horses, often cantering down the road, pretending to be a fine steed. But today was different. He told the teamster that he was in a hurry to get home to Mamma. The teamster jiggled the reins and the wagon rolled on. Hands deep in his pockets, Willie headed toward home.

Eight minutes later, one of his sisters, perhaps Charlotte, came riding along the road toward home, accompanied by a family servant. They met no one. At home, her mother was worried because Willie had not arrived.

By six p.m., the alarm had been sounded. The woods quickly filled with searchers from Commonwealth and Florence. The men searched the woods throughout the night: the mining area, test pits, ditches, swamps, and any out-buildings that might hold a clue.

Wednesday dawned cold with a light snow falling. The searchers were organized in more orderly groups, some on foot, some on horseback, and still others in wagons. Each group was instructed that the steam whistles at both the Commonwealth and Florence engine houses would blow at short intervals throughout the day. If Willie was found, they would signal with a succession of short blasts.

By Thursday, a call had gone out to area police. Captain Dickinson offered a large reward for information leading to the recovery of his son, dead or alive. The good citizens of Florence pledged a contribution, as well as the manager of the mine.

Around one p.m., a large group of citizens gathered at Juneau Hall to organize a more systematic search, determined to cover every piece of ground for clues. The searchers were divided into groups of ten, with a captain for each group. They stationed themselves about a rod apart and set out. The *Florence Mining News* stated that the search was so careful that a broad-axe which had been lost the year before was found hidden in the hollow of a basswood tree, covered with brush. But no sign of Willie was found.

On Saturday, a band of Indian trackers was called in. The search continued. The rewards were increased and family and friends were almost insane with worry and concern.

A week later, on Friday, December 11, a group of school girls on their way home were stopped by two men in a buggy.

"Which one of you is the Captain's daughter?" they were asked. The girls said she wasn't with them.

The *Florence Mining News* reported that "after some swearing, they disappeared."

The girls ran for home, hearts pounding, eyes wide with fright.

Clues and false leads came in from Chicago, North Dakota, Washington, Maryland, Virginia, Delaware, and Pennsylvania as the sad tale was picked up by a widening circle of newspapers. The Dickinsons checked all promising leads. Mrs. Dickinson traveled to many of the areas where the leads sounded the most promising. Eventually she visited every state in the nation.

On August 11, 1888, Willie would have been thirteen years old. The *Current* of Norway, Michigan, ran a story from Wausau, Wisconsin which began: "Dr. Kate Bushnell, of the Social Purity branch of the Women's Christian Temperance Union, some time ago visited notorious resorts near the city on her mission among fallen women. At one place kept by one Johnson she noticed a young boy stopping there. Growing suspicious she made inquiries."

Coincidentally, Dr. Bushnell later boarded the same train as the Dickinsons. She shared with them her story about her visit to the "Cotton Farm." After so many years of searching with so much disappointment, the Dickinsons were reluctant to pursue the lead. After all, the doctor had only seen the boy briefly. But later, after Dr. Bushnell had paid a visit to the Dickinsons and saw the younger children, she found their likenesses so similar to the boy in Wausau that she was convinced that he was Willie.

Dr. Bushnell returned to Wausau and again visited the Cotton Farm. She telegraphed the Dickinsons to come at once, and notified the local police. A raid and rescue was planned. Two policemen and a local clergyman set out for the Cotton Farm. On the way, they met a man on horseback who had warned Johnson and the girls of the raid, along with a few local citizens at the Farm who were sampling the wares.

The police sent the minister back to town for an arrest warrant for Johnson and four of his girls. When the police and clergyman arrived with the warrant, everybody in the house was fleeing through a corn field, making tracks for the nearest woods. The police nabbed them all and threw them in jail. Upon questioning, Johnson produced the boy. He said he had befriended the homeless boy from Canada, and had given him a job working on the farm.

Upon questioning, the boy said he had a sister named Christine. One of the Dickinson girls was named Christine. There were enough other similarities to convince the police that the boy was Willie. They sent word for the Dickinsons to come.

Mrs. Dickinson quickly arrived with her older daughter Lottie at her side. A *Milwaukee Sentinel* reporter was on hand to report the meeting. The women went to the Cotton Farm where they met with Johnson and the boy. The account said both the boy and Johnson told rambling stories that did not agree in the details. It didn't take Mrs. Dickinson long to discern this could not be her Willie.

The article stated: "As the house was full of people, which fact, the ladies thought, might have had a tendency to confuse the boy, they afterwards determined to talk with him privately. A quiet interview was easily obtained, and the result only confirmed the opinion that he was not Willie."

"Then you are sure that he was not your son?" the reporter asked. "If I had not been positive that he was not my boy, I would not have left him there," Mrs. Dickinson replied.

In her interview with the reporter, Mrs. Dickinson said she was sure that Willie had been stolen. She said she knew who his abductors were and the motive which prompted the crime. The article continued: "Evidence to prove this, and it will be proven when the proper time came, had been in her possession long since. She declared that while she might not live to see her boy again, she had firm faith that her children would some day see their poor brother."

In 1900, when Willie would have been twenty-five, clues were still coming in, according to news clippings gathered by William J. Cummings when he put together a history in 1985.

"Mrs. Dickinson became almost like the mother of the milk box missing child program, returning numerous children to their parents, but never her Willie," says Mike Moreska.

In 1898, Captain Dickinson was transferred. His daughter, Charlotte, went away to school in Boston. In 1889, she married the most eligible bachelor on the iron range, O. C. Davidson. He took his young bride home to Commonwealth where he was in charge of mining operations—to the same house where she had lived when Willie had disappeared eight years earlier.

Two years later Davidson was made superintendent of the Oliver mining properties in the Menomonee Range with headquarters in Iron Mountain, Michigan. They moved into the superintendent's home on the north end of Carpenter Street, now the Chippewa Club. There they raised four sons.

The Davidsons were over-protective of their children; the boys were always under constant supervision by either parents or servants. They were seldom allowed to leave the yard, although other children were always welcome to join them in play. The boys could choose between riding horses from the stables, bowling in the indoor two-lane bowling alley, or swimming in the pool at the back of the house. Recalling the strict supervision, one son later said he was sure it was because of the disappearance of little Willie.

Three full-time gardeners tended the extensive gardens, and acted as informal bodyguards of the children. Along with the house maids and other servants, the gardener-bodyguards lived on the third floor of the main house.

When the Davidsons moved to the home in 1901, it was the property of the mining company. In 1934, the family purchased it from the Keweenaw Land Association, Limited. O. C. Davidson died there in 1943 at the age of eighty-six. Two years later, Albee Flodin and William Lewis purchased it with plans to develop it as a private business and social club, the Chippewa Club. Mrs. Davidson continued to maintain an Iron Mountain address, but spent her winters in Florida until she died in 1957.

Those who know the story well, those who see the swaying chandeliers, or detect the aroma of bayberry in the upstairs bedroom, wonder if Willie followed his sister here. Mary Formell smelled the strong aroma of bayberry one November day. She walked around the bed and suddenly the aroma was there, without benefit of candle or scented spices in a dish. She was so startled that she walked out and found a maid to check the room. Mary asked her if the room was in order. The maid said, "Yes, but someone has been burning a scented candle. Bayberry!"

Mary knew there had been no candle. Then she paused to smile. "There goes Willie," she said.

Chapter 6
Black Bart

Stagecoach Road is a bit less scary since they moved the snowmobile trail. The stories began years ago, when unsuspecting buggy drivers suddenly tightened the reins and held on for dear life as their horses bolted and buggies careened toward the nearest ditch. Then, drivers of Model T's and other early automobiles felt unseen hands grip the steering wheels as their engines sputtered and coughed until they died along Stagecoach Road.

When the snowmobile trail was first mapped out from Hurley, Wisconsin, to Gene Kaurinen's Root Cellar Bar and Restaurant across the border at Marenisco, Michigan, local folks wondered if the planners had considered the legend of Black Bart. They weren't surprised when wide-eyed snowmobilers came in with tales of dead engines and unseen hands that suddenly steered them off the trail. It livened up the conversations around the big stone fireplace as newcomers listen to the tales of the morning Black Bart robbed the stage.

Black Bart was Reimund Holzhay, a 22-year-old German who had left his parents and four sisters in Thueringen, Germany, to try his luck in America. He stayed with relatives at Fort Howard in Wisconsin's Shawano County where he found work in a planing mill. Later, he was recalled as being a good worker who understood machinery.

Away from work, Holzhay was a loner. In his free time, he took off for the north woods of Wisconsin and Michigan's Upper Peninsula. He was soon a proficient woodsman. Finally, dissatisfied at the mill, he quit.

Then in April, 1889, a masked man stopped a stage in northern Wisconsin. He was dressed all in black except for a red bandanna covering his face and slouch hat pulled low over his eyes. Brandishing a Winchester, he demanded money and escaped back into the woods.

The stagecoach hold-up made big news because even robberies in the West were no longer common—the last had happened years before. For five months, the hold-ups continued across Wisconsin's north country. It was as though the gunman was possessed. He jumped trains, waylaid stagecoaches, and accosted pedestrians with guns drawn. Because of his attire he was given the name 'Black Bart.'

At four a.m. on August 9, the Wisconsin Central passenger train from Chicago was running north to Minneapolis. The passengers were peacefully sleeping. At the tiny town of Abbottsford, a masked man dressed in black jumped onto the train. Armed with a gun and wearing a big knife on his belt, he robbed the conductor, the porter, and one passenger. When the porter attempted to signal for help, Black Bart shot at him, but missed. Black Bart pulled the bell rope to stop the train. When it squealed to a full stop, he leapt off the train and disappeared into the early morning darkness.

Two weeks later, on Monday, August 9, 1889, H. M. Paddan and R. Rintane with the Montreal and National Banks of Chicago, D. Mackachor from First National Bank of Minneapolis, and A. G. Fleischbein of Ashland, Wisconsin, were on a train north for a long-planned fishing trip to popular Lake Gogebic in Michigan's Upper Peninsula.

The train stopped at the isolated Gogebic Station. A stagecoach would take them the remaining five miles through the forest to Lake Gogebic. From the south end of the lake, they could fish its thirteen miles of waters for its legendary great northern and walleye pike, the fighting muskellunge, black bass, lake trout, sunfish, and crappies. In nearby streams, they hoped to land rainbow, brown, and brook trout.

After leaving the train, Fleischbein climbed up front with the driver of the stagecoach. After storing their fishing gear and luggage, the other three men climbed inside. Day was breaking as the stage headed north on Stagecoach Road, winding through dense northern hardwood forests of maple, birch, and oak that were cut by sparkling trout streams. "The stage was running along at a lively gait through the deep forest," newspapers later recounted.

Just short of Lake Gogebic, the road made a sharp bend, causing the stage to slow down. It happened fast. At the bend, a dark figure stepped from the thick brush with revolver drawn. He pointed it at the driver, and in true Western style, shouted for the driver and passengers to throw up their hands. Then he demanded their money and valuables. All but one man raised their hands over their heads. Mackachor raised only one hand. With the other, he went for his gun. Black Bart saw the movement. The two guns spoke as one. Mackachor doubled over, with bullets in the face and through his leg.

The horses had bolted at the first shot. The driver cracked his whip to make a run for it. Black Bart fired again and again. Up on the seat beside the driver, Fleischbein took a bullet in the hip. Jolted, he fell forward. The stage careened down the road and the driver fought for control, but the wounded man pitched over the side and into the dusty road.

As the stage disappeared in a whirl of dust, Black Bart approached Fleischbein with gun drawn and ready to fire. Fleischbein pleaded for his life. Finally, Black Bart took the wounded man's pocketbook and gold watch and chain, and left him laying in the dirt, bleeding profusely. Emboldened, Black Bart walked down Stagecoach Road, ready to plunge into the woods at the sound of any carriage or threatening parties.

He need not have worried. Fleischbein lay bleeding in the road for three hours before anyone was brave enough to come to his rescue. They took him to a hospital in Bessemer twenty miles to the west. Mackachor was treated in Eagle River, Wisconsin, then was taken home to Minneapolis. Neither man was expected to live.

Wisconsin and Michigan newspapers declared that it was the work of Black Bart. Sheriff Dave Foley of Bessemer gathered a posse of twelve men and took off in hot pursuit through countryside that one paper described as: "Denser or more thickly wooded country than this never grew."

Following his footprints, they tracked Black Bart for five miles. At four p.m., a pack of bloodhounds with Indian trainers were brought in from Wisconsin's Bad River Reservation and put on the trail.

On Tuesday, Fleischbein, weakened from the heavy loss of blood, breathed his last. Mackachor was recovering in Minneapolis.

The Milwaukee, Lake Shore and Western Railway offered a $1,000 reward for information leading to the capture of the "highwayman." The announcement filled the woods around Lake Gogebic with bounty hunters and others (at least fifty men), searching for clues.

Meanwhile, the trail was growing cold. Eluding capture, Black Bart had apparently jumped a train and made his way to the small mining town of Republic about thirty miles southwest of Marquette. He checked into the Republic House and stayed out of sight. However, alerted by the all-points bulletin from Bessemer police, City Marshal Glade learned that a stranger was in town. Glade placed him under surveillance. He telegraphed Bessemer for more information, and waited tensely as the night slipped away.

Marshal Glade suspected his man might make another run for it. Finally, at seven a.m. on August 31, the Marshal decided he could wait no longer. Backed up by Justice of the Peace E. E. Weiser, the Marshal walked down the street toward the depot. Ahead of them, they spotted Black Bart, apparently preparing to jump the next train out. When Black Bart saw the lawmen, he tried to duck out of sight. The Marshal made his move.

He jumped in front of the stranger, and shouted, "I want you!" Black Bart reached for the gun that had been tucked out of sight in a pocket. But before he could draw, the Marshal lifted his arm high and hit him with his billy club. Black Bart fell, unconscious. They picked him up feet-first, and hauled him off to jail.

Upon searching him, they found three revolvers, three gold watches, four pocket books, and other stolen goods. One pocket book was Fleischbein's. In another, they found papers bearing the name of Reimund Holzhay.

With that, Black Bart confessed. In Republic, Bart was placed under heavy guard for the train ride back to Bessemer. In his confession, Holzhay blamed the robberies on his health. He claimed it all began when a horse fell on him, knocking him unconscious. "I haven't been the same since, especially in the head," he said. He claimed amnesia. He said he did not recall robbing the Gogebic stage, that when he heard gunshots, he ran for the woods to escape trouble.

Incensed, men organized a lynching party which was stopped by local police. On November 18, 1889, Holzhay was tried and the jury reached a verdict in forty-five minutes.They declared him guilty of the last stagecoach robbery in the nation, with a life sentence at hard labor at the prison in Marquette. Spectators thought the prisoner seemed dazed when he heard the verdict.

Early in 1913, Holzhay underwent an operation for the removal of a bone splinter that was pressing on his brain. With the splinter successfully removed, he was declared to be recovered from his criminal tendencies. On July 11, 1913, he was released from the Marquette Branch Prison after twenty-four years.

Where did Black Bart go from there? Stop by the big stone fireplace at the Root Cellar or other Lake Gogebic lodges when local folks are in a talkative mood. They have traveled the old Stagecoach Road when the hardwood trees leaned heavy branches tip-to-tip along the shadowy tunnel of trees. They have their own tales to tell.

Chapter 7
Hear That Lonesome Whistle Blow

When the woods are quiet and the wind is only a whisper in the pines, old-time lumberjacks stop in their tracks to listen. Something stirs. Is it the wind? A sound mixed with the roar of Tahquamenon Falls? Or could it be the lonesome whistle of a train still crying in the swamps of Michigan's Upper Peninsula? Could it be, after so many years, the runaway logging train of Con Culhane? Or is it the "Beautiful Lady" sobbing for her man?

The fighting Irishman Con Culhane fought his way from Canada to Michigan's Thumb when the land was new. He was grubbing out a farm when he married Ellen, a plump buxom woman whom he liked to call the "Beautiful Lady." Ellen said her man was too good to pull stumps all his life, and encouraged him to start logging at Port Austin along the Lake Huron shore. He built her a fine home that is now the Lake Street Manor Bed and Breakfast.

Around 1890, Culhane followed the tall timber north across the Straits of Mackinac to Michigan's Upper Peninsula. Near the mouth of the Tahquamenon River where it empties into Whitefish Bay, Culhane built Ellen and their son Billy another home which they called "The Whitehouse."

Ellen seemed to delight in Culhane's swashbuckling ways. People still tell stories of the Beautiful Lady holding a lantern high above her head while her man tied into a rollicking, free-for-all, no-holds-barred brawl. As camp boss, he felt duty-bound to lick every man in camp, if only to provide entertainment in the deep woods.

Culhane often greeted green lumberjacks with, "My boy, can you fight?" When a lumberjack unexpectedly proved to be much stronger than he appeared and laid Culhane out flat, fair and square, Culhane made him straw boss. "Any man that can fight, can work," he said.

The ruddy-faced Irishman admitted that his Beautiful Lady had a soft heart in her ample bosom. He accused old lumberjacks too disabled to work of being "Ma's pets." Sometimes, overwhelmed by the number of hangers-on, he would order them out of camp, only to hear later that Ellen had secretly brought them all back again. After he fired one 'jack, he said, "It cost me $5 to get rid of him, and I'll wager it will cost Ma $10 to bribe him into coming back."

Behind his jabbing fists and Irish temper, Culhane is said to have been less hard-hearted than he pretended. Every year, he sent a check for $1,000 to the hospital in Marquette, intended to cover the doctoring of any sick lumberjack. If that wasn't enough, begorrah, he'd send more!

Culhane believed in doing things his way. A chore boy new to the woods stopped his boss outside the door of Ma's Whitehouse one day.

"What time do I wake the teamsters, Mr. Culhane," he asked.

"Any damn time you catch them sleeping," he roared.

When a landowner sent an auditor to check his books, Culhane handed him a list of workers' names and a memo pad with brief notes on the number of board feet harvested over the past month.

"Surely that isn't all the books you have kept," the auditor protested.

With face flaming red in anger and fists clenched tight at his side, Culhane brought his shoulders up to full height. "Of course not," he said. "The rest is written on the barn door and the back of the blacksmith shop."

Culhane was bluffing. He could barely read or write. His Beautiful Lady wrote the checks. He laboriously signed them. As crews moved deeper into the virgin forests and away from the river, Culhane confided in his Beautiful Lady that he wished there was a railroad to haul the logs from the swamps to the river where they could float downstream to Lake Superior. From there, they could be rafted to markets in Muskegon, Detroit, Chicago, and the world.

The railroad arrived by barge from Lower Michigan. Culhane's men laid fifteen miles of rail along the Little Two-Hearted River. He named the engine "Ellen K" in honor of his Beautiful Lady. Some folks swore that it was plated with gold. Culhane stood beaming, fists on hips as the engine chugged in, pulling the first cars of logs along the rails and into camp. "Here she comes," he called. "She's neither sleigh nor wagon. She's Ma's machine."

Lumberjacks wielded cross-cut saws. Timbers fell. Trains rolled along the rails with their loads of logs. It was time to move deeper into the forest for more trees. Lumberjacks sat around the bunkhouse at night, wondering how Culhane was going to move his train, which now carried two engines.

"I'll drive them across the swamp," he boasted. Under his direction, crews laid rails in two-mile sections across the bog and muskeg. Driving the locomotives to the end of the line, he picked up the rails behind and laid them in front. Just south of Slater's Landing, he was stopped by the Tahquamenon River itself. Without a builder or engineer in the crew, Culhane and his lumberjacks sank hand-hewn timbers and built a trestle above the dark waters to drive the trains across.

Soon it was time for the great river drive down the Tahquamenon River, over the Falls, and to market. Upriver, the Tahquamenon was a lazy stream, flowing slowly between forested banks. The river widened above the Falls, turning shallow in great amber sheets along the sandstone shelf of the 40-foot-high and 200-foot-wide Tahquamenon Falls. There the river dropped into a boiling pool and pushed off downstream through deep-cut cliffs, the current trailing a flurry of boiling white bubbles. The lip of the Falls was irregular and jagged, shaped so that the current would grab logs coming down the river and plunge them straight down into the boiling pool below to splinter and break apart.

Culhane waited until the low water of August. From the shore, he anchored one end of a rope around a convenient tree and secured the other end around the waists of his chosen crew. Playing out the rope, they eased their way to midstream and the lip of the Falls. Bit by bit, with iron chisels and sledges they carefully chipped at the lip, reshaping it inch by inch at the critical points. Culhane directed from shore. Finally satisfied, he signaled them back to shore, and waited.

Tahquamenon Falls

Upstream, logs were released. They came floating around the river's curve. Catching the quickening current, they sped toward the Falls and straight into the newly-chiseled notch. Shouts echoed over the roar of the Falls as logs shot like a bullet over the edge and out beyond the dangerous pool before dropping to float on down the river.

Culhane kept his logging trains moving, traveling across the big swamp a few miles at a time, cutting logging roads, moving the rails before him. Then on Friday morning, June 26, 1903, Culhane climbed aboard the tinder of the "Ellen K" as the train chugged off through the forest. Four miles east of his logging camp at Sheldrake, he stepped across the cars to shout orders to the brakeman. Suddenly the train gave an unexpected jerk. Thrown off-balance, Culhane fell between the cars. Ma's machine ran over him, killing him instantly.

Almost a hundred years later, the landscape still carries the marks of the fighting Irishman: remnants of the old Culhane bridge, which paddleboat Captain Bill Kallio points out as he cruises tourists on the *Tom Sawyer* riverboat, a network of railroad grades, ruins of a Culhane dam at the mouth of the Little Two-Hearted River, old lumber camps such as Sheldrake, Emerson and Whitehouse Landing, and a notch carved in the lip of Tahquamenon Falls.

Old lumberjacks tales say the engines never left the swamps. Some say the engines slowly sank, swallowed up by the tannin-stained swamp: one of iron, the other plated in gold. And when the wind is hardly more than a breath whispering in the hardwoods and the pines, others say the trains are still running across the swamp, with Culhane himself blowing the lonesome whistle of the 'Ellen K,' trying to make it back to Whitehouse Landing, and Ma.

Chapter 8
Captain Greene and the *Delta Queen*

The mighty Mississippi River flows along the western boundary of Wisconsin, past red bluffs, through locks, with Prairie du Chien to the south, then La Crosse, and past river villages such as Pepin, Maiden Rock, and Diamond Bluff. At the small town of Prescott, the river makes a bend to the west for St. Paul, leaving the St. Croix Scenic Riverway to follow the Wisconsin border north.

These waterways and others of the Midwest have felt the paddles of Great Lakes Native Americans, European explorers, missionaries, fur traders, and lumbermen. Now barges vie for river space with speedboats, houseboats, fishing craft, and the boats of the legendary Delta Queen Steamboat Company.

With her distinctive single black stack puffing billows of steam, sparkling white paint, and calliope wheezing *Waitin' For the Robert E. Lee*, the *Delta Queen*, pushed by a giant red paddlewheel, rounds the bend filled with yesterday's memories. Those who know her best say that an extra passenger walks her decks.

Entertainer Phyllis Dale is one who has encountered her. Her experience began as pleasant dreams were fading from her sleep after an evening of piano-playing and singing in the Texas Lounge. The clock on the bedside table in her small cabin of the *Delta Queen* showed four a.m. Rising, the short blonde singer shuffled into her slippers and opened the cabin door to make her way toward one of the two bathrooms shared by the other twelve crew members occupying quarters behind the pilot house on the steamboat's Sun Deck.

Suddenly, without so much as the whisper of sound, a figure stood before her in the narrow companionway, so close Phyllis could have reached out to finger the folds in her long flowing robe.

"I almost ran into her," Phyllis says, her voice tense and her eyes darting nervously as she recalls that night in March, 1991. "She wore an old-fashioned long green velvet robe, with her hair piled on top of her head. I spoke, but she never answered or even turned her head to look at me."

Phyllis says the woman moved gracefully, seeming to glide effortlessly. Then, as suddenly as she had appeared, the figure vanished. Phyllis rushed down the hall and around the curve of the big smoke stack to the open deck. It stretched empty before her except for a lone watchman making his rounds.

"I called to Ronald the watchman and asked if he had seen a woman in a long green robe. He said he had just walked the entire deck from fore to aft. Nobody was up, nobody was there."

Back in her room, Phyllis tossed restlessly. "The hallways are narrow," Phyllis says. "I was standing at the end of the hall. She couldn't have come past me, because a door never opened."

At dawn, Phyllis woke with the same warm eerie feeling that she had felt a few hours earlier. She sought out the captain. "I told him that an odd thing had happened last night, that somebody had appeared in front of me in the hallway at four a.m. He didn't seem surprised. He asked if I had ever heard of the ghost of Mary Greene."

Phyllis was new on board. After a month on the sister ship, the *Mississippi Queen*, she had stepped onto the deck of the *Delta Queen* only five months earlier. She had been busy arranging numbers for her performances as singer with the riverboat band and piano solos in the Texas Lounge. There had been little time for ghost stories. But now she listened.

Mary Becker Greene was one of the first female captains to pilot riverboats up and down the mighty Mississippi river system of America's midwest. She was born in 1868. As a young lady, the blue-eyed, brown-haired girl attracted the attention of Gordon Greene who had taken to the river as a steamboat deckhand at the age of sixteen. After they were married, she joined him on board. The Greene's children grew up on the riverboats. Back then, no ghosts walked the companionways in the predawn hours. Only the beat of the engines broke the silence as Captain Greene's riverboat sliced the dark waters and willows along the muddy banks nodded slightly in the breeze as the boat made her way past sleepy towns.

Between family chores, Mary headed for the pilot house and took her turn at the wheel. She diligently studied the Mississippi River and its tributaries, learning from her husband to "read the face of the water," its currents and eddies, sandbars, snags, and limestone ledges.

In 1890, Gordon and Mary established their own line, the Greene Line Steamers, forerunner of the Delta Queen Steamboat Company. They joined numerous other lines operating up and down the Mississippi and its tributaries from St. Louis to Cincinnati and from New Orleans to St. Paul.

Paddlewheel steamboats carried passengers, freight, mail, livestock – anything requiring transport along the rivers. Some riverboats took on fancy airs, with music, dancing, river gambling, and wheezing calliopes announcing arrivals and departures as gentlemen in top hats and gowned ladies waved to friends on shore.

The Greenes ran such a line and at one time had as many as twenty steamboats on the river. In 1895, Mary won her river pilot license, one of the first women to do so. Captain Mary Greene stood regally at the gangplank to welcome passengers including presidents and common folks, grey-haired matrons in flowing skirts and wide-brimmed hats and kids with a Tom Sawyer gleam in their eyes. At times, passengers or crew dared address her as "Ma Greene," but it usually drew a frown. She preferred to be called Captain Greene.

After the death of Captain Gordon Greene in 1927, Captain Mary shouldered the burdens of the line, sharing responsibilities with her son, Tom.

That same year, two new steamboats began overnight runs between Sacramento and San Francisco. Talk of the grand new steamboats reached the river captains along the Mississippi. Sister ships, built in Stockton, California; they were said to be the finest of them all. Their hulls were fabricated on the River Clyde at Glasgow, Scotland, their machinery came from Dumbarton, and their wheel shafts and cranks were forged at the famous Krupp plant in Germany. Their four decks and cabins were constructed by American shipbuilders. Their hulls had been knocked down and transported by steamship all the way to San Francisco, and sent by barge up to Stockton for assembly and completion.

Overseeing the task was Jim Burns, "a tough Irishman" and master shipbuilder, who took two years to design and build the vessels. He did not scrimp on cheap sub-flooring and studs. Instead, the floors were made of straight-grain virgin oak harvested from the Oregon coast and the main deck was ironwood imported from Siam and "laid on the heaviest iron angles you ever saw," wrote Captain Frederick Way, Jr., in his book, *The Saga of the Delta Queen*. Mahogany and oak were pressure-steamed into columns for the master lounge.

In 1926, the *Delta King* and *Delta Queen* were christened. The showboats ran overnight excursions and freight up and down the Sacramento and Joaquin rivers. The royal pair were tourist attractions, building memories propelled by their giant red paddlewheels. However, the Depression soon stopped the laughter. Few passengers could afford the fare. The boats sadly made their way to the docks.

With the arrival of World War II, the two magnificent boats sailed again. Along with thousands of Americans, they were drafted into the U.S. Navy. The *Queen* was renamed Yard Ferry Boat 56. Over their shiny decks and up their walls went coats of drab camouflage gray paint. Their designated assignment was to ferry troops bound for war to the military ships anchored in San Francisco Bay, and to provide the last leg home for the returning wounded.

When peace came at last, the *King* and *Queen* were mustered out and were offered up for auction by the U.S. Navy. All the way up the Mississippi word reached Captain Tom Greene and his mother Mary. She was in her seventies then, but she was still making almost every trip up and down the river with her son. Her blue eyes were keen and her hands still firmly gripped the wheel. The Greene Line was in need of a larger boat. Tom wanted the *Delta King*. Captain Mary Greene agreed and he headed for California.

Although still covered with layers of military gray paint, Tom could see and feel the magnificence of the twin paddlewheelers. Both were impressive, but he wanted the *King*. On the day of the auction, bids for the *King* kept climbing. Tom bid as long as he dared, but still they rose. He lost! For $60,000 the *Delta King* was bound for Asia. The *King* was prepared for the journey, but the mighty boat did not make it past the Golden Gate Bridge. It sank in the harbor.

Then the *Delta Queen* went on the block. As her only bidder, Tom Greene purchased the *Queen* for $46,000. Much later, Captain Way described the telephone call that brought the news. Tom said he had just bought a boat. Captain Way anticipated the result. "It's the *Delta Queen!*" he answered excitedly. Later Tom enthusiastically wrote Captain Way describing his new acquisition: "The grand staircase forward of the dining room beats anything I ever saw, including the Waldorf Astoria. The builder tore it down twice getting it right, they say. The lady passengers could really peacock down that staircase in their evening dresses for the Captain's dinner."

The *Queen* was taken to a shipyard in Antioch, California. With the catastrophe of the *King* in mind, she was carefully braced and boxed "like a mummy," with every precaution taken to render the unsightly craft as seaworthy as possible. During refurbishing, workers discovered mementos from her service in California. They uncovered several closet-size spaces with coins, papers, letters, and streetcar tickets from World War II sailors.

"There are a lot of hidden void spaces still in the *Delta Queen*," says First Mate Mike Williams. "Workers tearing into the bulkheads found tiny rooms that no one knew were there." He said while replacing materials on the Texas Deck, workers once uncovered a six- by eight-foot room, empty except for signatures of the original workers scribbled on the walls.

During the outfitting for her sea voyage, the original designer and builder, James Burns of Oakland, California (then 84 years old) stopped by to visit her for the last time. Bracing

Delta Queen

strengthened her cabins. The paddlewheel had been removed and her polished decks were covered with rough unfinished wood. On an inspection sheet someone had noted her as a "seagoing barge." One observer called her a huge floating piano box. Asked how long the paddleboat would last, Burns said, "She will last Captain Greene through his lifetime and someone after him."

By the spring of 1947, the *Delta Queen* was ready at last. On April 19, 1947, Greene's own Captain Way was at the wheel when she was towed out of San Francisco Bay, under the Golden Gate Bridge, and into the open Atlantic. They made their way safely down the California coast, through the Panama Canal and up the Gulf of Mexico to the Mississippi River. One month and 5,261 miles later, they reached New Orleans.

Tom and his twelve-year-old son, Gordon C. Greene II, boarded her for the trip up the Mississippi and the Ohio Rivers. With a change of crews, the *Delta Queen* was bound for her home port of Cincinnati, Ohio. It remains her home port to this day.

After she was refurbished in Pittsburgh, the *Queen* shed her piano-box image and emerged with polished decks, plush lounges, and an ornate Grand Staircase; her Victorian splendor restored and cabins open to the river breeze. The paddleboat was ready for launch.

When she sailed on her inaugural passenger cruise down the Ohio River on June 30, 1948, to Cairo, Illinois, Captain Mary Greene was on board. Her figure had rounded to a grandmotherly plumpness. A filmy hair net held her tight waves in place. Her steps were strong, hands steady, eyes keen. The matriarch of the Greene Line felt an immediate kinship to this new queen of the river. From the first launch after restoration, the *Delta Queen* seldom left port without her.

Life was still not easy for the *Queen*. On an early trip out, her tiller line broke. Without the steel wire cable that connected the pilot wheel to the rudders, steering was impossible. The pilot struggled as he attempted to keep her on course and away from the banks, sand bars and other treacheries waiting to snare her. A bridge loomed ahead. The river grabbed the *Queen*, pulling her further off-course. On board, tension rose as captain and crew struggled for control as the river flowed high and fast. As the current grew stronger and the pilings of the bridge loomed dangerously near, the *Delta Queen* sped under the bridge—sideways. She had made it once more.

Captain Mary Greene lived aboard the *Delta Queen* in a stateroom on the upper forward deck. There was no mistaking who had the last word on control of the operations of the vessel. Historically, Mary chose to leave such troubles on the shore. She had never allowed a bar on any of the Greene boats, and even with the luxury of fine dining offered here, she wasn't about to make exceptions. No liquor!

"She wasn't a teetotaler," said one historian. "She liked her sherry, but she felt that if alcohol was allowed on board, it could lead to trouble with the crew."

Captain Mary aged, but continued to board the *Queen* with every departure. On the evening of April 22, 1949, among her fondest memories and trinkets in her cabin on board the *Delta Queen,* she breathed her last.

The *Delta Queen* lived on.

"This is one very unique steamboat that has somehow survived for over seventy years," the First Mate says. "During the beginning days of steamboatin', boats wouldn't last more than five years. Snags in rivers would cause them to sink, they would burn, or fall to other obstacles and hazards. Yet somehow something, a benevolent or protective spirit, has kept her safe."

Those who sail her and know her best credit the spirit of Captain Mary Greene. They may meet her on the open decks, spot her on the thirteen steps of the Grand Staircase. Passengers and crew talk about the things they see and hear: pictures on the walls shaking when the waters are calm, covers jerked off beds, tappings echoing from empty rooms, footsteps through the dark of night.

"When I saw her in the passageway, I didn't get a scary feeling, but a warm feeling," said Phyllis Dale. "She didn't rush toward me, and wasn't startled by me. Later her granddaughter told me that it was her Grandmother Greene telling me that she approved of my being on board."

The *Delta Queen* passed down to Tom, then his wife, Leitha, after his death in 1950. Changes came to the River. Although Captain Mary Greene had fought it for so long, Leitha felt that the wants of modern travelers necessitated the addition of a bar and lounge. She added them adjacent to the dining room. The remodeled *Queen* took to the rivers again.

Crash! Fog swirled over the river, but there was no mistake. The *Delta Queen* was hit. A barge splintered her hull and came right through to the service bar of the new lounge! The name of the towboat pushing the barge was lettered bold and bright: the *Mary Greene.*

Captain Gabriel Chengary is Master of the *Delta Queen* today. He has sailed with her for twenty-nine years. Passengers have often talked to him about the sounds and voices they hear in the middle of the night. "Some people are more susceptible to the spirits. I have never seen the spirits myself, yet I try to keep an open mind," he says. He added that the members of his crew who have seen things are level-headed people, and not prone to imagine things.

While the spirit is normally peaceful, crew members said she can turn cantankerous and ornery if they're not looking after her boat. "She threw a cream pitcher at me!" one says on wonder. "We were in dock. There was no movement on board. I was rifling through a china storage cabinet, searching for Captain Mary's river license. I remember muttering, `Where in the world could those papers be?' Suddenly the inside door of the overlapping closure slammed open, knocking open the outside cabinet door. Out sailed a cream pitcher right past my head. I backed away. `O.K., Captain,' I said. `I'll leave it where it is.' I've never looked again."

The stories are numerous. Late one night the purser's office received a call from an elderly passenger who complained of being very cold and not feeling well. They dispatched someone to check on her. There was no response to the knock at her door, so they entered with their master key. The cabin was empty. A check of the boarding list showed that the cabin was unoccupied for the cruise. On another occasion a passenger called to complain of being ill. When a purser brought her hot soup and an aspirin, she waved him away.

"Oh, don't bother, young man," she said. "Someone was here already. The nice elderly woman told me to get plenty of rest, and everything will be all right." The purser asked for a description of her caller: she was matronly, plump, short of stature, piercing blue eyes with dark hair puffed around her face. No such person was on the crew.

Mike first stepped on board as a fifteen-year-old in 1981. He grew up in the old river town of St. Louis, working as a kid on other sidewheelers that made short runs up and down the river. On days when the *Delta Queen* was due, he would show up on the docks early to hear her calliope playing.

"I knew it was where I belonged. She was calling me even then," he says. "It wasn't just the boat; I felt that something was embracing me. She embraces me still, as long as I take care of her boat."

Beginning as a carpenter, he spent many long hours at night working on the boat alone, especially during winter lay-up. One such night while tied up at the Avondale shipyard, he was living on board in order to make periodic inspections for leaks that might invade the hull after her extensive repairs.

At two a.m. one stormy night, Mike was going through the forward cabin when an uneasy sense swept over him. "I could hear the murmuring of voices. They were very definitely human voices, talking at a low level from I knew not where."

No one was allowed on the boat at that hour. Mike walked the decks, searching for the voices. He was standing in the forward cabin lounge, listening intently above the rain and thunder, with only a dim light illuminating the area, when suddenly a loud slam echoed through the boat. "It frightened the hell out of me," he says.

He was convinced that it had come from an inside cabin door opening into the lounge. Mustering up all his courage he started walking in that direction. "I didn't see or hear anyone. The whispering had stopped."

With his master key, he searched every cabin on the boat, looked under every bed, in every closet. Finally, Mike headed back toward the Texas Deck staircase. The murmuring came again from behind him, like two people in hushed conversation. In response, he headed back toward the aft cabin. The murmuring stopped. "Finally, I gave up. I returned to my cabin and to bed. It was an uneasy sleep that night."

One night in1985, Myra, the chief purser was working late in her office off the cabin lounge. Suddenly she was swept with the sensation of being watched. She turned to the small window overlooking the deck. Peering in through the window was the face of an old woman: a pleasant, oval face with her hair held in place by a filmy net. The face slipped away and toward the cabin deck. Myra rushed out. The deck was empty.

Later Myra and Mike fell in love and married. "Ma Greene knows we're connected," he said. "She's watching over us. She's telling us to take care of the boat together."

More recently, crew members bunking in the mid-hold were wakened at five a.m. to the shrill cry of a woman's wails. She seemed somewhat distant, and yet near. At first they shrugged it off. But after being awakened morning after morning, several female crew members approached the Captain. He sent deck hands around to see if someone was trapped in an unused compartment. Was it a piece of machinery grinding into a wail? A malfunctioning fuel pump? The crew checked the tanks, and even listened to the bulkhead with stethoscopes, but found nothing. Finally the noises stopped, without providing any answers.

Karen "Toots" Maloy, riverlorian (historian) on the *Mississippi Queen*, said she has given the ghost all kinds of chances to show herself, but she never has. "You can want to see a ghost as much as other people, but it may not happen. Somehow I think you must have the ability to feel and see before it can happen to you," she says.

The closest she ever came to a "happening" was while working with a television crew on the *Mississippi Queen*, bound for Natchez, Mississippi. The *Delta Queen* pulled in and tied up alongside. The TV crew asked Toots to do an interview about the ghost on board the *Delta Queen*. She agreed.

The crew moved their equipment into the forward cabin lounge. They set up all their lights, and placed Toots before the cameras. They were ready to roll. "O.K., when I point to you, start talking about Mary," the director said.

The signal came. Toots said, "Mary Becker Greene . . ." and every light in the cabin blew out.

"Darn, we blew a breaker," someone said.

"Maybe," said Toots. "Or maybe she doesn't want us to talk about her today."

Another camera crew discovered its own mystery while covering the annual Great Steamboat Race between the *Delta Queen* and *Mississippi Queen*.

The cameraman requested permission to film in the Betty Blake Lounge at two a.m. when no passengers would be walking around to interfere. To include the Greene family, he scanned their portraits on the wall. First, the cameraman focused in tight on Captain Gordon C. Greene's portrait. Then he swung the camera to Captain Mary Greene's portrait. At that point, the cameraman leaped back. Great beads of moisture popped out on his forehead and he began to shake and tremble.

"What's wrong," the director asked.

The cameraman's mouth wordlessly moved up and down. With a shaking finger, he pointed at the camera. The director stepped forward and looked through the view-finder. He, too, jumped back. "She's alive!" he shouted. "Her eyes are alive."

He quickly swung the camera to the other pictures, then back to Mary. "The rest are only portraits, but she is alive."

The crew did not go to bed that night. Without further filming, they huddled together in the forward lounge until daylight reflected off the river. Then they scurried off the boat.

Crew members who have grown accustomed to her presence feel only benevolence—as long as they pay attention to the boat. They feel Captain Mary might get a little nasty if things don't go to her liking.

For one *Delta Queen* crew member, all this ghost hogwash was a little difficult to believe. A routine U.S. Coast Guard inspection was coming up, and the bright young Chief was tense. He pushed the crew as they readied for the inspection. Gently, Mike suggested to him that if he stopped and 'petted' the boat, she might do more for them.

"The boat is a mechanized nonentity with nothing spiritual about it," the Chief snapped. "When something breaks, an engineer is here to fix it."

They worked on. The following day, the inspection was ready. But as the Coast Guard inspectors made their rounds, everything that had been readied was undone. Later, the Chief approached Mike and said, "I'm beginning to believe you. Tell Captain Greene she's got another friend on the boat."

Captain Mary seems to approve of the latest refurnishing. Her mahogany and teak woodwork glows, and the natural grain of oak along the deck is almost as smooth as a piano. In the public spaces the decor is Victorian, with fine carpeting and ornately-carved furnishings upholstered with plush tapestries. The glow of Tiffany-style lamps and chandeliers softens the sheen of the overhead beams. The beds in the cabins along the main deck are covered with comforters in burgundy and blue that capture the sunlight through stained glass windows. The cabins on the top decks are furnished with antique chests and brass beds covered with quilts.

Delta Queen

Mike enjoys walking around the boat at night after things are quiet, touching her walls, listening from the aft cabin lounge. "She is like my cantankerous old grandmother who knew what was right with me when I didn't know. She takes care of me still," Mike says.

A master carpenter once said that an old wooden boat is like an old wooden house. Many workers pound the nails into the wood, hammering it down, storing up its energy. Over time, the energy seeps out, releasing some of the energy of the people who built it and the people who spent so many years living in it or loving it. On the *Delta Queen,* Mike and many other members of the crew feel there is always a little bit of the energy coming out. "Instead of touching a cold piece of wood, it is body temperature," he said.

Mike advises interested passengers to discover her personality by walking her decks. The engine room is the body of the boat, with the original solid oak pitman moving back and forth, beating like a heart. Her breath is the steam rising from her stack, propelling her north along the Wisconsin shore.

"During lay-up when she is under repairs with mess all over her decks, she is resting, sleeping. At these times with no distractions except the boat herself, she talks," Mike says.

Chapter 9
I May Know That Ghost

When John and Lois Findlay moved into Small Point Cottage with their seven children in 1971, they were so busy with the big house, new school, and all of Upper Michigan's Mackinac Island to explore that they paid little attention to the Amish hex sign hanging over the refrigerator in their new kitchen.

Tall cedars throw dark shadows at Small Point Cottage, crowding thick around the wraparound veranda with its view of Lake Huron. During the busy summer tourist months from June to mid-September, bed and breakfast guests fill the rooms. Lace curtains hang at tall windows. Overstuffed couches, chairs and family pictures spread the feeling of a relaxed, warm, and friendly place.

Through an archway, a long hardwood table dominates the dining room. A glass-fronted china cabinet stands in a corner; a sconce with electric candles is mounted on the wall. Glass teardrops dangling from a chandelier capture the light and scatter jeweled patterns around the room.

Each morning guests gather for a continental breakfast of freshly-baked pastries, cereals, bagels and cream cheese, and fruits spread on the buffet. Occasionally guests inquire of the Findlays about noises and footsteps heard in the night. The Findlays only exchange glances and a smile. When the spirit's antics annoy the guests, they give him a good scolding.

However, some of the island's year-around residents take the happenings more seriously. "Some refuse to come past the cottage in the winter," Findlay says. In the long cold months of winter, the rocky point is covered with snow and the waves on the lake are silenced by thick ice. "Some island snowmobilers even circle onto the frozen lake, rather than take the road that runs along the front of the cottage."

Mackinac Island deals kindly with its ghosts. Its heritage goes deep, all the way back to Indian spirits and the legends of their god Manitou who they believed moved back and forth from his home beneath the waters through the gateway of Arch Rock, a limestone formation along the shore. Soldiers killed in the War of 1812 lie buried under white markers in the military cemetery.

Small Point Cottage was built in 1882 along the foot of East Bluff a few hundred yards west of its present location. A sister house was built next door. Over the years, the sister house was torn down. Small Point Cottage, then known as the Old Turner Cottage, was moved to the east side of Old Mission Point resort where it now stands.

Small Point Cottage was known as the 'spirited house' long before it was converted to a bed-and-breakfast inn. Lifetime-island resident Sarah Chambers, who for years was recognized as Mackinac Island's matriarch, often told stories from her childhood. She had kept letters written by girlhood friends inquiring of the spirits that brought mischief to the three-story home that first stood on the lower slope of East Bluff. Over the years she shared her stories with its various owners. After the Findlays moved into the house and a Detroit paper wrote about the ghost, Mrs. Chambers urged her son to drive her to Small Point Cottage in one of his horse-drawn carriages. "I'd better get out there and see that ghost," she said. "It may be somebody I know."

In 1971, John Findlay accepted a teaching position at the Mackinac Island Elementary School, and moved his family north from Indiana. The brick school for children of the 600-year-round residents stands on a low rise off Lake Shore Road overlooking Lake Huron.

"Small Point Cottage was the only empty house on the island that was insulated in winter and big enough to hold all of our seven children," Findlay says.

On their first Saturday at Small Point Cottage, the ghost came to lunch. "We had all the family downstairs when I heard someone walking upstairs," recalls Lois. "At first I thought it was the dog, but I looked around and there he lay. Then I thought the cat might be playing games, but I remembered he was in the basement."

She asked the kids if they had brought a new friend home for lunch. Nobody had. They investigated the sounds. Nothing could be found.

Throughout the school year, the Findlays learned to expect such noises. They loved the house on the point, spirit and all. Then toward the end of the school year, Findlay accepted another teaching position. Because they could not bear to leave Mackinac Island altogether, they purchased Small Point Cottage and now spend the summers with their spirit. As the children grew up and one by one their bedrooms became vacant, the Findlays decided to convert the house to a summer tourist home. Guests returning year after year became like old friends. Lois started serving morning coffee, then pastries with the coffee, and the tourist home evolved into a bed-and-breakfast inn.

The spirit continues to roam about, sometimes making nightly noises, sometimes going through the entire summer season without a show of mischief. He seems to prefer rattles and bangs over actual encounters and appearances: a rattle at the door, an echo of receding footsteps down the hall. Female employees have become so accustomed to the sounds that they felt the spirit needed a name. They affectionately called him 'Aaron.'

Sarah Chambers had told the Findlays that the spirit was that of a young girl who had lived in the house many years past. When her parents decided to move away, the girl was devastated. She vowed she would never leave. On their day of departure, the girl was nowhere to be found. The parents searched and searched and finally found her hiding in a small closet off the upstairs hall.

Other islanders tell of a long-ago owner who also loved the house. When work took him back east, he left reluctantly, looking back over his shoulder until disappearing from view. He was dead within thirty days.

Yet the cause of the disturbances remains unsolved. Findlay said nobody was killed in the house. Nobody died there. No catastrophe struck it.

Lois calls Aaron a 'gentle spirit.' "He is mischievous. He likes hiding things in unlikely places. Things appear that were never there, and suddenly they are," she says. She also confesses that at times when she walks down the back hall and reaches a certain point, she feels an almost overwhelming urge to cry.

One guest inquired about which of the Findlay children walked in their sleep. "None,"the Findlays replied. "One does," the guest insisted. "He or she kept walking up and down the hall half the night. I hate to complain, but I couldn't sleep."

Sally North, wife of Michigan Senator Walter North of Sault Ste. Marie, was the fill-in hostess at Small Point Cottage for seven summers, taking over when the Findlays returned to Indiana and school. She says the mischief seems to center around Labor Day when the Island is crowded with bikers, runners, and high-energy guests. "When we got really busy with too much TV, too much music, too much excitement, mischief often comes along," she says.

For some reason, the ghost was very interested in keys. A large oak desk in the living room was the center of the Findlay's domestic life. Early in their occupancy, the desk key began to disappear and reappear in the most unlikely places. One day they discovered the desk was locked and the key was nowhere to be found. Findlay pried the desk open with a pocket knife and found the key inside. He then completely dismantled the desk but found nothing unusual.

Finally Lois hid the key in a wineglass on a china cabinet shelf. "He didn't find it there for the longest time," Findlay says. When Lois rearranged the china cabinet and moved the wineglass to the kitchen, the desk key disappeared again. "Aaron was up to his tricks again," Findlay says. It was later discovered behind the candle on the wall sconce.

In addition, the spirit began to play with a crystal pendant from the dining room chandelier. One morning after breakfast, as John was dusting the dining room chairs, he found a pendant laying on a chair seat that had been occupied by a guest only a short time before. The pendant was identical to the ones dangling from the chandelier above the table, except for the bright shiny electrical wires at the end.

Looking up, he saw that the wires on the other pendants still attached to the chandelier were rusty with age. He searched the chandelier for the missing spot to reattach the fallen pendant, but found no vacant spot. Calling in the maids, he offered $5 to the person who could find where the pendant should be hung. Finally, they gave up. All the pendants were in place.

"Then the pendant kept disappearing and reappearing. After that season, we took it home to Indiana and hung it in the window as a sun catcher. It hasn't gone missing so far," Findlay says.

While the spirit prefers to stay out of sight, Findlay says the most incredible sighting was made by the two young sons of guests. "We had told the parents none of the stories about the spirits," Findlay says.

One evening, the Findlays were babysitting the two young boys whose parents were off hiking around the Island. The oldest of the boys looked up at John with big round eyes, and said, "I got scared last night."

The young boy said a man had been in his room. Findlay assumed he was speaking of his father. "No, that other man," he said. "I don't know who he was, but he was sitting in the air smiling at me." The boy said he woke his little brother, and they watched the man until he drifted away.

"Did you wake your Mom and Dad?" John asked.

"At first I didn't. Then I did, but the man was gone and they didn't see anybody. They told me to go back to sleep, but I couldn't." Findlay was bothered that the boy was frightened by their friendly spirit. He probably just needed another scolding like in 1979, during the filming of *Somewhere in Time* on

Mackinac Island, when John heard the front door lock click three times. He didn't move from his chair or lay down his newspaper. "Leave the door unlocked," he scolded to the empty room. "We have guests out tonight without a key." He insists that the spirit responds to such scoldings. "He never bothered the front door again," he laughs.

Sally North is still puzzled over the foreign exchange students and the loud music coming from the third floor. One summer two English boys, nice young men, were living upstairs. But they loved playing records as loud as they could on an old-fashioned phonograph. "On a particular evening when their music was much too loud for the other guests, I called up stairs to tell Clive that he should turn it down. But it was still too loud," Sally explains.

Sally climbed the stairs to deal with the problem head-on. As she explained to Clive again why he must turn down the volume, the phonograph arm suddenly swept across the record in a screeching motion as though pushed downward by an unseen hand. "The record was gouged all the way across. We saw it happen," Sally says in amazement.

She said she always felt that the spirit liked her. She was not afraid. "But I often wonder about it. On a dark night during a power outage, when it is foggy out and bats are flying around the island, would I really have spent the night in the house alone?"

At the end of each season, the Findlays head home to Indiana. The winter caretaker makes regular calls to Small Point Cottage, checking water pipes and handling any necessary maintenance. On one such call he entered through the basement door as usual, leaving the front porch and gallery carpeted smooth with snow. He was working in the front section of the basement when he heard footsteps on the porch. He assumed his children had followed him. The front door creaked opened, and the footsteps moved into the living room directly above his head.

How did those kids get through that front door? he wondered. "Come on down," he yelled. "I'm working in the basement."

A footstep scraped along the entrance hall heating grate, and then there was silence.

"Here I am, down here," he called again as he bounded up the stairs. As he reached the hall, he stopped. It was empty. The door was shut. Rushing to the window, he looked outside. The porch was smooth with last night's snow, and no footprints tracked it up. He ran through the house, searching.

No one was there.

Friends inquire of the Findlays about calling in an exorcist. "No way!" they insist in unison. "That would get him mad at us."

Chapter 10
I Did Not Eat Charlie

Most nights Angelique Mott woke up screaming. She was awakened by the ghost of Charlie, his reddened eyes staring at her intently as he sharpened and sharpened and sharpened his knife on the worn whetstone. She dreamed of the cold shores of Isle Royale during the winter of 1845, of Lake Superior with its waves silenced by thick ice, and the gut-wrenching hunger that stretched on and on and on.

Mercifully, some nights she dreamed a kinder dream of the day she met Charlie Mott (also known as Charles LaMotte), the strong French-Canadian voyageur who strode down the long dock and into her life on Madeline Island at LaPointe, Wisconsin. He was dressed like the other voyageurs, a red woolen cap pulled at a rakish angle over his thick hair.

He was strong from hours and days at the paddles and from shouldering packs at portages across the north country. The muscles along his thighs tightened and relaxed with each step of his deerskin moccasins. He saw Angelique standing at the end of the dock. Their eyes met. The dream ended, and she slept.

LaPointe was a prosperous trading post and village at the southwestern tip of Madeline Island in the Apostle Islands when Charlie's long freighter canoe crossed Lake Superior from Sault Ste. Marie. Catholic and Protestant missionaries ran the missions and the schools. The red store and warehouse of the American Fur Company was prominent among the four or five white clapboard homes, in contrast with about forty-five unfinished houses of fishermen and voyageurs, and the forty Chippewa lodges nearby.

Angelique and Charlie had not been married long when the 54-foot, two-masted schooner *Algonquin* owned by Cyrus Mendenhall pulled into the harbor. As one of the first sailing vessels on the Great Lakes, she warranted attention. She was sleek, fast, and seaworthy. In 1845, she had sailed up the St. Marys' River to Sault Ste. Marie. For the next three weeks, she was tugged and pulled by teams of oxen over timbers and rollers laid on the portage around the mile-long Soo Rapids. Then she sailed along the south shore of Lake Superior, stopping to drop off supplies at trading posts along the way, including LaPointe. Aboard the *Algonquin* were copper prospectors from Detroit. They had heard of the legendary copper deposits on Isle Royale, and they were anxious to reach it. The Motts were invited along.

Isle Royale is a beautiful Michigan island a full day's sail on Lake Superior from LaPointe. It is forty-four miles long and ranges from between four to nine miles wide. A spiny ridge of copper-bearing conglomerate covered with moss runs down the middle, and pockets of marshes and lakes are scattered throughout the thick forests of spruce, fir, cedar, and mixed northern hardwood. Its shoreline is cut by scenic bays. Offshore are hundreds of timber-covered islands, boulders, and reefs. Over 3,000 years ago, unknown miners dug copper from open pits, leaving no evidence behind except stone hammers and scattered tools.

The *Algonquin* set sail with the Motts on board. Years later, Angelique told her story to newspaper reporters. "After landing, I wandered a long way on the beach until I saw something shining in the water. It was a piece of mass copper," she said.

The prospectors grew very excited, and struck a deal with Charlie and Angelique to hold the claim in their names. To remain on the island for the summer, they would pay Charlie $25 a month; Angelique would get $5 to stay and cook. The thought of long summer days alone together on the island was pleasant. They accepted. But first they wanted to accompany the men back to Sault Ste. Marie for supplies.

"There I first met Mendenhall, the man who brought us into all this trouble," Angelique said. Mendenhall already had a reputation for trouble. He had ventured to the north country as a trader of furs and fish for the American Fur Company. By 1840, he was obsessed by the stories told at trading posts of mass copper deposits along the Lake Superior shore. In his rush for wealth, he not only dabbled in copper mining, but tried to rush things along by changing American Fur orders. In 1844, American Fur Company notes and correspondence record illegal changes the trader had made in supply orders bound for trading posts, both in quality and quantity for the delivery of inferior trade articles. Later, the company attached Mendenhall's furs to cover his debts. The records include a copy of an agreement for payment signed by Mendenhall.

Mendenhall quit the fur trade business and invested in copper mines on the Ontonagon River as well as buying the *Algonquin*. He asked for and won a contract with American Fur Company to transport goods, but they kept a close eye on him.

Mendenhall had told the Detroit copper prospectors that to transport so many provisions so far up the lake would be very expensive and troublesome. He said that earlier in the season he had already shipped more than they could possibly need to LaPointe. Both food and supplies, he said, were only a 24-hour fairweather sail from Isle Royale.

Algonquin Captain Lewis W. Bancroft, his four-man crew, the prospectors, the Motts and Mendenhall set sail from Sault Ste. Marie for LaPointe. They caught sight of Madeline Island in late June. Rounding the tip of the island, they made safe harbor. Mendenhall went for the supplies only to find that his shipment had not arrived.

It seemed that voyaguers had already passed through and replenished their own supplies. The shelves at the fur company and the missions were almost bare. They were able to purchase only six pounds of rancid butter that had turned white like lard, a few beans, and a bit of salt. The mission promised half a barrel of flour; they could spare no more.

Nobody wanted another trip back to Sault Ste. Marie, the nearest source for goods. Yet the prospectors could think of nothing but the unguarded copper laying on the beaches and in the ancient pits at Isle Royale. They pressed Charlie to go to the island to hold their claim until they could make the run up the lake for their supplies.

Angelique gazed across the waters and worried. She was loathe to leave LaPointe and her mother, her friends, the mission where she had gone to school, and the church where she had adopted her Christian faith. "I didn't want to go to the island until we had something more to live on, and I told Charlie so, but Mendenhall over-persuaded him," Angelique said.

They could fish for trout along the rocky shores, he said, and take the canoe he would provide into the bays. Mendenhall promised that he would send a bateau of provisions in a few weeks. At the end of September, well before the arrival of the snows of winter, he would return and take them off the island back to LaPointe and home. "So, very much against my will, we went to Isle Royale on the first of July," Angelique recalled.

Charlie and Angelique stood on Isle Royale's rocky shore as the *Algonquin*'s topsails disappeared over the horizon. They were left with meager supplies, their personal belongings, a birch bark canoe, and a fishing net. They set up their camp on Rock Harbor along Isle Royale's eastern shore, on the shores of what is now Mott Island, headquarters of Isle Royale National Park.

During the first few weeks, life was good. The summer sun leaped suddenly from wide Lake Superior from the east in the morning—the direction from which the supply bateau would come. The evening sun lingered long in the sky before finally ducking behind the spiny ridge that forms the backbone of Isle Royale. Together, the Motts built a cabin and gathered wood for their fire. They roamed the bays and inlets together. They often discovered copper. Fishing was good. After a day's catch they paddled back to their island where Angelique roasted their meal over glowing embers.

As the weeks wore on, the summer warmth burned away by late afternoon and evenings grew crisp. Berries were ripening on the slopes and they scavenged with small animals for their share. One day in late summer, the winds lashed at the trees and the skies poured great rains that swelled the streams and soaked the moss-covered rocks and boulders. Angelique and Charlie huddled inside their cabin until the pounding turned to a patter, then a drip, drip, drip.

When they ventured outside they were shocked to find their canoe was gone, snatched from its mooring and washed into the inland sea. They tried to fish with the net, but without the boat it was soon cut to shreds. Nothing was the same after that. They began to keep a careful count of the days and weeks. Angelique watched anxiously as the autumn washed the forest summits in blazing reds and golds. The chill that came with the night now lasted throughout the day. Birds were gathering, chattering from the boulders before they flew away.

"Oh, how we watched and watched and watched but no bateau ever came to supply us with food; no vessel ever came to take us away, neither Mendenhall's nor any other," Angelique recalled.

The flour sack was empty. The butter was long since used up, and now the beans were gone. With no canoe or net, they could catch no fish. They were near panic, daring not to consider an entire winter isolated on the island without food.

The snows came and Angelique ardently wished for the snowshoes back in LaPointe. Bit by bit, wave by wave, the harbor froze, and finally the lake as far as they could see. Now Charlie and Angelique had to skim the ice from their water hole when they wanted to drink.

Angelique watched her Charlie grow weak; the muscles in his thick thighs seemed to grow thinner with each coming day. She thought of herself back home at LaPointe, wearing beaded pantalets, a smooth broadcloth shawl wrapped about her shoulders, and moccasins beaded with porcupine quills on her dancing feet.

The berries were growing bitter now, but they ate them anyway, along with bark and whatever roots they could dig from the frozen ground. When Charlie could no longer dig, Angelique dug harder, clawing around the cabin like a wild animal as she searched for anything they could boil in water to satisfy the gnawing hunger. Some barks and roots seemed to make the hunger worse, but they could not help but eat them. "Hunger is an awful thing. It eats you up so inside, and you feel so all gone, as if you must go crazy," Angelique said.

Five days before Christmas, the shelf was bare except for a small amount of salt. Temperatures dropped until even the fire couldn't keep the cold away. Snow came like a swirling mass hour upon hour, banking deep around the shelter, covering paths and boulders until all was white. They sat beside the fire aching with hunger.

A few months earlier, both the Motts had been known for their strong bodies. Around campfires along Lake Superior, men told tales of the tall Indian maiden and her enormous strength. Once a Frenchman wagered she could not carry a barrel of pork to the top of the village hill and back. Angelique shouldered the barrel and marched up the hill without a pause. She turned around and marched back down, dropping the barrel at his feet. "Now," she said to the Frenchman. "Climb on top and I'll carry it back up again."

But on Isle Royale she was spent, and without a supper to give her Charlie. As a voyageur, Charlie had paddled freighter canoes, and could lift and carry nine hundred pounds of furs across slippery portages secured by a strap around his head. Without food, Charlie meekly sat and waited. His face was red and his body burned hot with fever.

"One day he sprang up and seized his butcher knife and began to sharpen it on a whetstone. He was tired of being hungry, he said, he would kill a sheep—but something to eat he must have. And then he glared at me as if he thought nobody could read his purpose but himself. I saw that I was the sheep he intended to kill and eat," Angelique said.

Charlie sat before the fire, eyes red from the fever, hunger and madness. He tested the knife against his finger and sharpened and sharpened and sharpened. The day slipped into night shadows. She dared not sleep, with Charlie sitting beside the fire with the knife in his hand, watching her every move. She could almost feel the blade at her throat, and expected him to leap upon her at any moment.

Finally, as the fire turned to embers, his eyes blinked heavily and his head nodded. Seizing her chance, she sprang at him and wrestled the knife from his hand.

Afterwards the fever seemed to leave him for awhile, and he appeared not to remember the knife. She was so grateful that she never mentioned the awful day and night around the fire. She tried to protect him from her agony. Soon he couldn't move from his bed. She brought water to moisten his lips. She shifted his body to ease the pain. Although he was so thin, she sprained her arm trying to lift him.

Through the long days and nights she seated herself behind him so he wouldn't see the tears that flowed down her cheeks when she saw his bones through his shirt. His breath came in short gasps, then whispered breaths through still lips. Then he died.

Angelique grieved because she had no coffin. What could she do with Charlie? She broke the ice from the water hole, heated it over the fire, washed his body, and laid it out like she had learned at the mission. "How could I bury him when all around it was either rock or ground frozen as hard as a rock? And I could not bear to throw him out into the snow," she said.

For three days she sat with Charlie in the hut, tending the fire, remembering the good times. Then she began to worry. What if her fire spoiled Charlie? She must move, and take the fire with her! Nearby Angelique started her own lodge, digging away the snow, breaking off limbs and fashioning them into a shelter. She often winced with pain from the sore arm, but she continued to build. At last it was ready. Waiting for the wind to die down, she carefully moved her fire and left the cold cabin to Charlie.

Fire was all she had left. She was obsessed with keeping the flames going, grabbing at every twig and branch—anything to feed the fire. "Oh that fire, you don't know what company it was. It seemed alive just like a person was with me, as if it could almost talk, and many a time, but for its bright and cheerful blaze that put some spirits in me, I think I would have just died." Once she fed the fire too high and the hut caught fire. She put it out with snow.

She tried to sleep away the hours and days, but soon she could hardly sleep at all. Although the spirits danced in the Aurora Borealis, Angelique was not afraid. "Sometimes it would be so light in the north that it was like a second sunset, then the night seemed to turn into day. But I was used to the dancing spirits and was not afraid of them. I was not afraid of the Mackee Monedo or 'Bad Spirit,' for I had been brought up better at the mission than to believe all the stories that the Indians told about him."

In the loneliest hours, she visited Charlie in his hut. And she prayed. In the night came the demon that would haunt her the rest of her life. "Ugh! What a trouble it was! The worst trouble of all . . . Sometimes I was so hungry, so very hungry, and the hunger raged so in my veins that I was tempted, oh, how terribly was I tempted to take Charlie and make soup of him. I knew it was wrong; I felt it was wrong, I didn't want to do it, but I feared that some day the fever might come on me as it had on him, and when I came to my senses I might find myself in the very act of eating him up," she said.

Angelique knew she could stand the hunger and the loneliness, if only this one great fear would just leave her. When the nagging fear pressed the hardest, she prayed. When she prayed hard enough, an answer always came. One time she had gone more than a week with nothing to eat but bark and her fear of not being able to resist eating Charlie was overwhelming. The next morning, she opened her door. "I noticed for the first time some rabbit tracks. It took away my breath and made my blood run through my veins like fire," she recalled.

Angelique frantically tore at her dark hair, pulling out long strands. With trembling hands, she plaited the hair into a snare. She chose a spot and carefully set the snare, praying that she would catch a fat one and catch him quick. Finally she heard the familiar cry of a rabbit. She rushed to it, grabbed the animal and with frantic motions tore off its skin and ate it raw. She set the trap again, but despite her efforts it was another week before she caught another. With half her hair gone, she continued to make snares and catch rabbits through the winter.

Hemmed in by ice, snow, and drifts, she sat for hours before the fire until her arms and legs grew too stiff to move. "So at last, like a bear in a cage, I found myself walking all the time." By the end of February, the fiercest storms were behind her.

In early March, Angelique made her way down the shore. A small boat that had been washed up by the waves lay half-buried in snow. She set to making it water-tight. She tore part of the sail into strips and wove them into a fish net. The ice made it difficult and dangerous to reach open water to fish, but anything was better than sitting and waiting. She landed a few.

The days and weeks passed. The snow and ice melted slowly. "Soon the little birds began to come and then I knew that spring was coming in good earnest. God indeed had heard my prayer and I felt that I was saved. Once more I would see my mother," Angelique remembered.

One morning in May she went fishing early and netted four mullet. She paddled back to shore, tossed more wood on her fire, and started cooking her fish for breakfast. Through the silence she thought she heard the echo of a gun. Startled, she almost dropped her pan. There it was again! It was a shot! She leaped up and tried to run to the shore, but the excitement was too much. Her legs gave way and she fell to the ground. With pounding heart, she looked toward the east and saw a boat!

She was waiting for them when they landed. The first one off was Mendenhall. He put out his hand to Angelique. She took it.

"Where is Charlie?" he asked.

Angelique said, "He is asleep. You might go up to the hut and see for yourself." Mendenhall and the rest ran for the smokeless cabin. Angelique waited. They found Charlie dead. Suspecting Angelique, they investigated but it quickly became clear that Charlie had obviously starved to death.

Later, Angelique would tell how she had reproached Mendenhall and he had begun to cry and try to explain why he had not come. "He said that he had sent off a bateau with provisions and didn't see why they didn't get to us, but the boys told me it was all a lie." She left Mendenhall to live with his own conscience.

The boat took Angelique back to LaPointe and her mother and friends. Before she made her way to Sault Ste. Marie where she died in 1874, she worked for awhile for the Amos Harlow family of Marquette. Legend says she was a good worker, except for her dreams and the demons that visisted her in the night. They could hear her calling over and over, "I did not eat Charlie! I did not eat Charlie! I did not eat Charlie!"

Chapter 11

The Ghost of Woods Hall

The mood was tense during final's week at Northland College in the late 1960s as the students crammed for algebra, English, science, and philosophy exams. Finals were also on the mind of the disk jockey as he worked late in the small cramped student radio station on the top floor of Woods Hall. The DJ should have been at the library cramming or in his room reviewing his notes like the other students, but this job was important to him. It felt good to know that the music he was playing on the old-fashioned turntable was helping his fellow-students stay awake, providing a soothing background for built-up tensions from studies.

He knew the ghost stories circulating around the campus, as did all the other students, especially as they related to Woods Hall. They were told and retold every semester. But he had never seen anything and he only occasionally heard the late-night footsteps that were said to sound in the corridors of Woods Hall.

Students tell of a shy freshman residing in Woods Hall in the 1920s. He constantly rambled on to his classmates that he did not meet his wealthy father's expectations. His grades were lagging and his leadership skills were faltering; he felt that he was failing in everything he attempted. When September was gone and the leaves of October began to fall slowly to the ground he finally realized that he would never pass. Thanksgiving lay ahead, with his father carving the turkey and the family gathered around the table. All eyes would turn on him and his father was sure to say, "Well, son. How are thing at college? Knocking them over with your high grades like your father did in school?"

He did not go to the Halloween Dance. What girl would go with him? He was a nerd. In despair, he paced the halls. Finally, in the basement of Woods Hall, he found a rope. He tied it around a beam, looped it around his neck and jumped.

Tonight those stories crossed the DJ's mind. Perhaps it was the wind sweeping in strong gusts across Chequamegon Bay, rattling the windows, crying in the trees. As he chose his line-up of music for the night, a temporary lull in the wind revealed a groaning sound like a rope under a heavy load chafing on a beam. The DJ froze, his hands in mid-air. There it was again! And then above the music, he heard footsteps coming down the hall, shuffling softly, closer. They stopped at the door, then moved on. Seconds later they returned, shuffling, stopping, then shuffling closer.

The footsteps stopped at the station door.

"It's nothing," the DJ said in a hoarse whisper. "My imagination is just running away from me." Bravely he called out, "Come in." The door knob turned. The door slowly opened.

The doorway was empty, except for the sound of heavy breathing. The DJ bolted, jerking open the window, climbing onto the fire escape and dashing down the steps in a furious clatter as though pursued by a thousand demons.

Inside the station the turntable continued to spin and spin and spin.

Woods Hall was torn down the summer of 1970. Some say the ghost moved to another building and still walks the halls when the wind blows in stormy gusts across Chequamegon Bay.

Chapter 12
Lotta Morgan: Woman of the Night

Lotta Morgan attracted all eyes on both sides of the social ladder when she hit Hurley, Wisconsin, in 1886. Before many days had gone by, they were calling her the prettiest woman on the iron range. She walked with grace, her shoulders back and head held high. She bubbled with boundless energy and enthusiasm, eager to meet the day and party most of the night, as intelligent as the cream of the society, yet ready to share laughter with the coarsest of the miners and lumberjacks.

Men crowded into the Central Garden Variety Theatre to watch her perform and curry her favors. She dressed in fancy clothes and lacy gloves. She wore diamonds. Girls in the bordellos called her a lady, while suspecting her of luring away their wealthier customers.

A hundred years later they talk of her still when a shadowy figure of a woman in a billowing ankle-length skirt and fringed shawl is seen darting from one of the late night bars that still line Silver Street. High school children write essays about her. Area historian Larry Peterson tells her story. Writer Ray Maurin of Ironwood, Michigan, wrote a play that was produced in the local playhouse. Balladeer Jackie Lutey sings the story of the dastardly deed that "done her in." Edna Ferber came to town to research the character of Lotta Morgan, then wrote of her in her famous novel, *Come and Get It*.

Hurley was new and wild when Lotta (or Lottie) Morgan came to town. Newspapers from Milwaukee to Detroit referred to it as a "sinkhole of corruption" and "that toadstool called Hurley." Another wrote that the hottest places in the universe were Hayward, Hurley, and Hell.

Hurley was fourteen miles inland from Lake Superior in a rugged hard-to-reach area cut by wild rivers and dense forests and only the barest hint of trails. The logging industry reached Hurley around 1870, with lumberjacks harvesting the giant white pine to build American cities and decorate the palaces of Europe. Rich deposits of iron were discovered in quantity in 1879.

In 1884, Nathaniel Moore and the Hayes brothers hacked a trail through the forest and around boulders. They hauled in primitive equipment and started digging for iron in an open pit. Others followed. On December 3, the first saloon opened its doors.

When the train tracks were laid on January 1, 1885, the town consisted of one frame building, two log cabins and a tent. But with the train, folks were ready to move in. The first general store and a second saloon opened in March, two hotels were up and running by July. Soon saloons along Silver Street ran all the way to the Montreal River. Still they came: miners, saloonkeepers, bartenders, bordello girls, bankers, families, storekeepers, ministers, school teachers, politicians, doctors, and morticians.

Looking to formally establish the new town, citizens turned to attorney Michael Angelo Glen Hurley of Wausau, Wisconsin. They approached him with empty pockets and the suggestion that for his legal work, they would name the town for him. Glen Hurley, Wisconsin, was born. In 1886, the name was shortened to Hurley.

On September 26, the town's first child was born to Mr. and Mrs. John Wallace. In tribute, the founding fathers proudly presented the parents with a building lot. Two weeks later, John publicly declared that the baby was not his. He packed Mrs. Wallace and somebody else's baby off on the next train.

In October, 1885, John F. Sullivan opened the Dew Drop Inn saloon on Silver Street. The town was rollicking. A woman attending a social dance on Silver Street asked a young man to see her home, but later he wasn't sure he should have been so gallant. The woman's husband started firing just outside their front door. The escort escaped with bullets flying around his head. The husband was arrested, then released on bail.

The town boomed. Silver Street soon boasted wooden sidewalks although its streets were dust in summer, frozen with hard-packed snow in winter, and bogged down with wall-to-wall mud in spring and fall. Men covered with black ore dust swarmed in from the surrounding iron mines. On payday, lumberjacks from camps on both sides of the Wisconsin-Michigan border stomped their hobnail boots against saloon floors, gambled, and then tromped upstairs to see the 'ladies.' When it was over they limped back to the woods with empty pockets, broke until payday rolled around again.

When Lotta Morgan stepped off the train in 1886 with her showgirl figure, plumed hat, lace collar, and long skirt billowing around her high-button shoes, she found fifty-four mines going strong along the Penokee-Gogebic iron range between Wakefield, Michigan, and Upson, Wisconsin, with Hurley right in the middle. Lotta found a town wilder than any western cow town. Hurley's base population of 3,000 swelled to 8,000 when the miners and lumberjacks came to town. Bars, brothels, and gambling halls lined Silver Street and the side streets that sloped down to the Montreal River, growing wilder all the way down. Businessmen had tunnels dug under the river to Ironwood on the Michigan side for easier access and escape from raids.

Saloons followed a pattern: long ornate bars with a variety club stage on the first floor where men could meet the girls, gaming rooms in the basement with escape doors and hatches, and the 'parlors' on the second floor with tiny cubicles where the girls entertained. One bordello boasted a hundred such rooms. The town provided other distractions as well. Hurley's twenty-ninth saloon opened in July. If that wasn't enough, folks could cross the Montreal River to Ironwood where there were twenty-seven more.

Hurley was never dull. A boozed-up miner charged into the Germania Mine office, knocked over a teamster and timekeeper and ripped off the bookkeeper's moustache. The fact that he objected to his small wages did not save him from arrest.

In August, a telegram was sent from Hurley to a Mr. D. Dix, with the sad news that his son Clarence had died. Send burial money, the wire said. Instead, the senior Dix sent his son-in-law to personally arrange the funeral. Before checking with the mortuary, he stopped at one of the local saloons for a drink to steady himself for the task ahead. Sitting on the next stool was Clarence!

Fire hit Hurley on June 27, 1887. By the time the fire wagon could get up steam, it had spread out of control. Thirty-five buildings including saloons, markets, hotels and stores burned to the ground. One newspaper said, "Hurley is a very sorry sight."

Less than two weeks later, fire hit the Alcazar Variety Theatre with showgirls and other theatre people trapped upstairs. Ten people died, all friends of Lotta Morgan. At the funeral, a vocalist sang, A*sleep in Jesus.*

By August 11, Hurley had become a very quiet town, with no prostitution, excessive drinking or gambling. Ten days later, the "great moral revival of Hurley had all but collapsed." New buildings and trashy dives were re-opening all along Silver Street and other streets as well. D. P. McNeil was busily working on his new saloon, the Marble Hall. Its floors were marble and its wainscoting polished Italian marble with its woodwork painted to match. The bar and fixtures were of polished mahogany and other fine woods. Ornate glass mirrors were imported from France.

By March, 1888, the town had been completely rebuilt. Some building sites in the seedier districts were only fifteen feet wide to allow realtors a greater profit. There were fifty-two saloons in Hurley alone. In May, a bartender was taken insane and died. Probable cause: bad booze. Electric lights were installed along Silver Street. Joe Sheehy opened a saloon in the building formerly occupied by the YMCA.

Lotta was born Laura Whitley in Arkansas on April 14, 1861. Sometime in her girlhood, her family moved north. Lotta smoothed her hill-country edges at her uncle's Park Variety Theatre on Chicago's State Street. In 1882, she and Pinkerton Detective Smith moved from Chicago to Milwaukee. For several years they lived as man and wife at 418 Broadway. Then she caught the train for Hurley alone. Although she soon took up with Sullivan at the Dew Drop Inn, she also rented her own room on Silver Street.

Lotta found work in Hurley as a variety show actress. Her voice was slow and easy with a honey-dripping Arkansas twang. She was an instant hit with miners, lumberjacks, businessmen, and bankers alike. After the last show she visited the playhouses and saloons along Silver Street, flashing her diamonds and her smiles and stuffing dollars in her fancy purse. Some claim she was one of the girls working the houses after she finished at the theatre, while others whisper behind their hands that her forays with distinguished gentlemen of the town were just for fun.

"She was always well dressed, always had plenty of money, and was a figure very prominent in the circle to which she belonged," said a minister at her funeral.

During the early morning hours of September 21, 1889, across from Lotta's room on Silver Street, the Germania Mine payroll of $39,160, along with other monies, bank notes, gold, and silver was taken from the Iron Exchange Bank. The town was in an uproar. Detectives hinted that they had strong clues about the whereabouts of the robbers.

On November 7, three arrests were made: assistant bank cashier Phelps Perrin, retired saloonkeeper Ed Baker, and a woman known as Lou Thayer. Lotta Morgan was subpoenaed as witness for the defense. The townsfolk were scandalized when Lotta left town. Folks speculated wildly about what Lotta may have seen from her window across the street, or what she may have learned from pillow-talk. The controversy had barely calmed down when Lotta was back in town.

Hurley now boasted eighty saloons and even more bordellos and gambling rooms. Lotta resumed her appearances in variety shows and hitting the saloons after her evening performances. But something was apparently bothering her. She appeared uneasy. She began carrying a pistol in her purse.

On Thursday evening, April 10, 1890, she made her usual rounds of the local saloons, laughing with the girls, teasing the men. Later, neighbors heard her stirring around in her room across from the bank. Then she left. She stopped by John Sullivan's saloon. At 11:30 that night, she left through the back door that opened onto the alley between Silver and Cooper streets. Mrs. Onum who lived nearby heard a shot, then heard someone run past her window. She peeked out. From the dim shadows cast by the electric lights along Silver Street, she watched a person dart away.

Early on the morning of April 11, elderly Joe Flandrena cut through the alley toward his house nearby. He stopped in his tracks! A woman lay in the snow behind Svea's Saloon only steps from Sullivan's back door. Blood covered her head and the front of her dress. Blood had seeped into the snow around her, turning it a crimson red. Her purse lay at her feet, with a pistol nearby. It was Lotta Morgan.

They found her lying on her back with her dress saturated in blood. Her body was cold to the touch. An ugly four-inch gash was directly over her right temple. The *Ironwood Times* printed that "the body was weltering in blood from two nasty wounds to the head."

At the crime scene, police found that nothing had been taken from her: her diamond rings were on her fingers, her jeweled necklaces around her neck, and her money in her purse. They determined that the pistol at her feet had not been fired. It was her own.

Lotta's body was moved to the undertaking rooms of the Ragan Brothers. There the doctors determined that death had come from strikes on the head by the blunt edge of an ax or hatchet. The gash across her face was administered as she lay on the ground. They also found a bullet wound in her chest.

Word spread like lightning.

At nine o'clock in the morning, a reporter from the *Iron-wood Times* arrived. He talked to police and bystanders, sur-

veyed the crime scene, and took a casual look along the alley. In Crocker's woodshed fifteen feet from where the body lay, the reporter found a small broken axe, old and badly nicked. Blood stained the blade and handle. It was laying as though tossed there by someone in a hurry. Police determined it to be the murder weapon.

Justice Blackburn immediately impaneled a jury to conduct an inquest. It began at nine o'clock on Saturday and lasted until Monday morning. Its findings were death by two blows from an axe, delivered by an unknown assailant, either of which could have been fatal.

On Monday, small handbills edged in black appeared throughout the city announcing the funeral of Lotta Morgan at the Opera House at three o'clock. "Everyone is invited to attend," the handbills stated. And they did. All classes—upright citizens and bordello girls, lumberjacks, miners, ministers, bankers, and saloonkeepers. A third of the crowd were women. By one o'clock, the large Opera House auditorium was packed, with standing room only and others turned away at the door. Newspapers declared that curiosity had attracted more people than the most honored citizen could have gathered. Three local ministers officiated, "doubtless guided by the belief that it would give them an opportunity to reach a class never seen in the pews of their churches."

At three o'clock, eight prominent citizens bore her casket down the aisle and placed it near the stage. The Presbyterian church choir sang. Rev. C. C. Todd delivered the eulogy. "I knew Lotta Morgan," he began dramatically. "With all her failings and all her sins, Lotta Morgan was no ordinary woman." Lotta would have loved the minister's tributes: "ladylike," "possessed with a woman's heart," "kind and courteous," "always with aspirations for something better," "she could have adorned a high social position," and "strong religious inclinations." He recalled that at the funeral of the girls who died in Hurley's Variety Theatre fire three years earlier, Lotta had been deeply moved by a solo, *Asleep in Jesus*. They sang it for her again.

Then to the sinners, he admonished: "I blush to say that in this town people say that houses of ill-fame are a necessary evil, that they are good for the business of the community. But oh, my brethren, do you wish prosperity and business at such a price as this? Do you want dollars to come into your place stamped with a woman's blood?"

Lotta was "borne to the cemetery grounds south of town and buried with all due ceremony." It was her twenty-ninth birthday.

Newspapers across the country picked up the story. The *Detroit Journal* called Hurley the sink of corruption, a self-made pest house for the unclean. "Let her revel in the name that has been brought upon her by a majority of her citizens," the paper continued. "To her murdered harlot she pays more homage than to her most worthy citizens, while her murderer stalks at large."

A Wisconsin paper called for justice: "There seems to be a disposition on their part to have the matter hushed up . . . That Lotta Morgan was an abandoned woman of the town is no reason why her slayer should go unpunished."

The police turned up a bloody coat and arrested its owner. Then they released him with little explanation. Some folks around town blamed the murder on a jealous wife. Others suspected that it was linked to the Iron Exchange Bank robbery of 1889. "She must have known something. She could see everything that went on from her room across the street."

Rumors and speculation flew.

"Remember when that Pinkerton agent Wappenstein came to town to investigate? He suspected that retired saloonkeeper from Ironwood was in cahoots with Phelps. I think he heard that Lotta was sleeping with him on the side, and questioned her about the robbery."

"I heard that she discovered some of the bills under Phelps pillow, and he told her about it. Police arrested both of them, and then let her go."

"When she got that subpoena to testify for the defense, she left town. Mighty suspicious! And now she is dead."

The town continued to party. By the turn-of-the-century, there were 101 saloons, fourteen whorehouses and five gambling operations. But over time, Hurley changed. Across the Michigan border in Wakefield, Dick Swanson built the Regal Country Inn and dedicated some of the rooms to historical characters. Room 2 has easy access to the lobby; the name across the door plate reads "Lotta Morgan." The decor is Victorian as Lotta would have liked it: decorated with an antique sleigh bed with curved footboard, cherrywood parlor set, scrapbook containing newspaper clippings of her murder, and a penciled sketched portrait of Lotta on the wall.

Today all the mines are closed. Tourists stop to see the high tin ceilings in the twenty saloons that remain, along with the handful of strip tease joints. No one recalls when the shadowy figure first appeared along Silver Street and the alley in the back.

On some summer evenings, the Hurley Chamber of Commerce sponsors cultural walking tours and a variety show, with local volunteers playing the main characters that gave the town its reputation of ill-fame. Sometimes on such nights, the shadowy figure of a woman in a long flowing skirt can be seen moving through the alleys, sometimes darting briefly under a street lamp as she crosses Silver Street. Near the shadowed doorway to one of the saloons, the figure stops to listen. From inside drifts the plucking of a guitar and a clear soprano voice:

Hey Lottie, Hey Lottie, Hey Lottie, Hey lay.
Who made love to Lottie on Lottie's last day?
Hey Lottie, Hey Lottie, Hey Lottie, Hey lie.
Who knew that Lottie was going to die?

Chapter 13
The Memorial Day Visitor

The teller of the tale nervously twisted her fingers around her coffee cup, turning it between her hands, scraping its rough base against the cheap pottery saucer in the small restaurant outside of Mercer, Wisconsin. Rain splattered against the window pane. It was a warm summer rain, but it suddenly seemed cold as she told her story. Someone pushed open the door to the outside and a rush of cold air swept through the room.

It began in the early 1920s when the town's telephone system was located in the operator's living room. The few business phones were all one digit. The telephone operator was popular in town, knowing most everyone's business but keeping it to herself.

"She smiled and giggled and cared," the woman across the table said. "She was well-respected. She would not tell a lie. She believed that lightning would strike her if she told a lie." One Memorial Day, with few calls coming in, the operator took a walk to visit her mother who lived in a small house directly across from the town cemetery. As was her custom, she entered the front door without knocking. She stopped in her tracks!

In one of her mother's favorite living room chairs sat a woman dressed in a long flowing skirt, tight jacket, large hat, and gloves, clutching a beaded purse. Without moving, she silently stared out the window.

The operator rushed into the kitchen where she knew her mother would be working. "You have a guest! Who is she?" she asked.

Her mother turned to her with wrinkled brows. "No, I don't," her mother said.

Consumed by curiosity, the two women rushed into the living room. The chair stood empty. No one was there.

The operator described the woman she had seen, the period clothing, the hat, her hair.

Her mother shook her head. "I accepted no one into my home, but I have seen such a person at a grave in the cemetery across the street."

Later, relating the story to friends, the operator explained it away. "If it was a spirit, she knew she was safe in my mother's home."

They never saw the woman again. But others have, it is told. Some say that in the early years before the rail lines were abandoned, the woman could be seen every Memorial Day getting off the train from Milwaukee.

Some believe her to be the spirit of Eleda Benson. Some say that in the 1940s and 1950s, such a woman started coming north on the train to lay flowers at her parents' graves. She was slight of build, with small round glasses, a slight dimple in her cheek, and brown hair caught back in a bun. She always came during the daylight hours and always on Memorial Day.

By 1980, the train no longer ran through Mercer. But several "reliable witnesses" still saw the woman in the cemetery. Some said she appeared dressed in pink during the summer months, and black in winter, kneeling at one grave, and then the other.

It is said that some respected citizens of the community experienced other encounters with the ghost, but they refused to speak of it. "I know what I know, I know what I saw, but I'm not putting my name to it," one said.

The woman across the table drained her cup. She watched the rain run down the window pane. Memorial Day had passed. She fished around in her purse for her car keys, pushed open the door and headed home.

Chapter 14
The Crying Cabin

The great-grandson of a mighty Indian chief may have been considered a good catch for some men's daughters, but Horatio Seymour had his mind set on royalty of another strain.

Before the turn-of-the-century, Seymour fretted about rearing his family in the wild untamed north woods of Michigan's Upper Peninsula when his uncle, the governor of New York, asked him to go west to manage the family interest in the Michigan Land and Iron Company. Seymour and his proud wife were accustomed to a more genteel way of life than that offered by the brawling lumber and mining town they found at Marquette, Michigan in 1882. Not even the elite of Ridge Street measured up to the expectations of the couple who counted presidents and near-presidents among their ancestors.

A small dark man in fragile health, Seymour built a house in the best part of the city overlooking Lake Superior. Beyond the spacious gardens, and behind the fretted scrolls and hedged windows, the proud and queenly Abigail Adams Seymour, descendant of John Adams and Abigail Smith, shunned all social functions among the "base pioneers" of Marquette. She refused to bow to northern fashions or allow Mary and Horatio, Jr., to play with children in the town. She sent them back east for their education.

When dark-eyed Mary returned from eastern schools with her younger brother, the Seymours feared that her bubbling friendly spirit might attract some of the local youths into thoughts of romance and matrimony. To protect them from influence of local society and youth, Seymour built a cabin at the base of Sugarloaf Mountain along the shore of Lake Superior several miles west of Marquette. The summer Mary was seventeen and "Rakey" fifteen, the ailing elder Seymour took them over the old lumber road to the summer cabin at the cove. Mary lifted her heavily starched skirts and skipped along the moss-cushioned path toward the cabin. The strong low-roofed cabin of hewn logs nestled in a dark stand of virgin spruce and hemlock, its wide porch opening toward a jutting point of granite, which formed a natural cove and protected it from the inland sea. The girl nodded to a tall handsome bearded man with fierce steady gaze hired as their guardian and caretaker.

He was Henry St. Arnauld, known as 'Santinaw,' pioneer land-looker and outstanding woodsman of the north. Santinaw was descended from Mamongesida, who had led a party of Indian warriors for two thousand miles from LaPointe, Wisconsin, to Quebec, where they fought in the ranks of Montcalm on the Plains of Abraham. His great-grandfather was Waubojeeg, chief to the Ojibway's Reindeer Clan, and his father was the French-Canadian fur trader Edward St. Arnauld who had married Marie Des Carreaux, granddaughter of Waubojeeg.

Santinaw, at fifty-two, was straight as an arrow, swarthy, tall, and strong beyond the strength of normal men. He was swift of foot, a woodsman who knew intimately every growing thing in the forest and every fish that swam the streams. For years, he had roamed the forests for weeks on end, living off the land. When he came back to town, he headed straight for a barber for a careful trimming of his long flowing beard and straight dark hair which fell across his shoulders. Only then did he hurry up the hill to his two-story home on the edge of town where his wife and family were waiting.

Then death struck. Twice. He buried a daughter and four years later, his wife. Santinaw lingered in Marquette through the summer of 1898. Even though his other two daughters were almost grown, he was reluctant to leave them so soon after the newest grave was dug under the pines. Nor was he ready for the forest. When Seymour offered him the guardian job at Cove Cottage, a despondent Santinaw accepted. He found some measure of contentment with the lake lapping at the sandy stretch of beach down the path or pounding out its fury against the boulders, with the wind whispering in the trees and the mountain to flex his muscles upon.

The Seymour youngsters were avid pupils of nature. For three summers, Santinaw returned to the cottage to tutor Mary and Rakey on the lore of plants, herbs, and trees. Long hours slipped away as they hiked the animal trails and scaled the highest boulders and hills along the lake.

Seymour's health continued to fail and he was soon confined to a wheelchair. Occasionally he ventured his chair along the packed ruts of the logging road that approached the cabin, or pushed up the trail leading to Sugarloaf as far as the incline allowed.

"Would you like to see the top?" asked Santinaw as he watched Seymour gazing upward. The little man considered the rugged mountain strewn with jagged boulders, and shrugged. Santinaw found a way. For days he hacked through the underbrush and trees, clearing a path that skirted boulders and spanned rock cuts. On Seymour's next trip to the cove, Santinaw tied him to the wheelchair and pushed it all the way to the top.

Meanwhile, Mary had blossomed into a young woman. With the lonely Santinaw the only man in her life, Mary fell in love during the summer of her twentieth year. "I pressed myself on Henry," she said in later years.

He shook his head in disbelief. He protested the difference in their ages; the still-handsome Santinaw was fifty-five. "My ways are Indian ways," he said.

"Then your ways will be my ways," she insisted.

Finally in October, as the forest glowed rainbows of crimson, orange, and gold, she persuaded him to run away with her. Henry said they should catch the train for Houghton eighty miles west where they could be married.

Mary scribbled a hasty note to her parents and left it pinned to a sewing cushion. Her father found it and stopped the train. Word of his daughter's choice of husbands had already reached

Marquette. The entire town held their sides and laughed behind their hands. Too good for their sons? Royalty, indeed! Mrs. Seymour fought against the marriage to the end. There was no forgiveness from Mary's stern father. He insisted they go through with it and banned his daughter from his home.

Santinaw took his bride to his house in town. Although it was a comfortable two-story home, it was outside the social circles. Santinaw's daughters tried to teach their youthful stepmother to cook and perform other household chores. Mary tried, neighbors recalled. Even after the birth of their baby girl, she tried not to complain when Henry's work took him to the woods for weeks on end.

At least Rakey and the rest of Marquette's youth profited from the marriage. The socially inclined and even the Seymours said if rigid rules could produce such a marriage, it was time to reevaluate. There was an immediate clatter of lowering social barriers.

Two years later, Mary heard that her father was very ill. The family was returning east. Mary stayed.

In 1905, the Seymours knocked at her door with word that her father was dying in New York. He was begging for Mary. She must come at once.

Her Henry was in the woods. What should she do? She could not leave a personal note. Henry couldn't read. Finally she packed baby Marie's clothing and without a note or farewell to Henry, headed for her father's bedside. When Santinaw returned, his wife and child were gone.

Seymour lingered on for eighteen months before he died. By then, Mary's resolve to return had weakened. Her family pleaded for her to stay with them a while longer; Marquette was no place to raise a little girl. Mary enrolled in McGill University, and later Syracuse, studying the Indian language and poring over plant lore she had first learned from Santinaw. Perhaps she could share these things with Henry when she returned.

Later her mother died, leaving a large inheritance to Mary and granddaughter Marie, who was becoming a young lady.

Santinaw's daughter rejected her Indian blood and heritage, forbidding her mother to speak of her father or the past.

"I didn't want to grieve her, so I refrained," Mary later said.

Marie made the matrimonial match her mother had missed, becoming the wife of a prominent New York attorney.

For awhile, Mary pursued her studies while working at the Smithsonian Institution in Washington, then headed west again. For five years she wandered across Wyoming's deserts and mountains, collecting plant specimens and studying Indian lore. Years drifted past. She often thought of her husband along Lake Superior's shores.

Twenty-five years after she had left his house in Marquette, she tore open a letter from Henry's niece, Mrs. Peter Clyne, of L'Anse. Mary's eighty-four-year-old husband was dying. When the family told Santinaw that Mary was coming, the old man's shoulders sagged. "Why, after all these years?" he asked.

A portly matron descended the steps of the train and hailed the village's only taxi for the short trip to her husband's side. She knelt beside him. "I have always loved you, Henry," she said to the white-haired old man. Henry reached out to clutch her hand.

The Clyne household was already overflowing with relatives. Mary found a room with cousins two doors down. She visited her husband daily, often scolding him for not taking better care of himself, and especially for his grooming habits. Each morning Santinaw splashed his head and beard with water until they were dripping wet, then walked outside in the freezing cold to empty the wash basin. He would step back through the door with hair and long flowing beard frozen stiff. "You'll catch your death," she said. But Santinaw stubbornly continued his grooming rituals.

He remained handsome and straight as an arrow until the end. He regained some measure of health and lived for almost three years after Mary's return. Following his death, Mary lingered in the area that she had deserted so many years before. She rented an apartment in Marquette, bought a sailboat, and sailed down to the cove where she had fallen in love.

In 1934, Mary Seymour St. Arnauld walked past the gingerbread house overlooking the bay where her parents had lived, then stopped at the smaller house where Santinaw had taken her as a bride. She wondered if anyone had ever understood her, if she had understood herself, or why she had stayed away so long.

There was nobody left to understand, except perhaps young John Tobin, the new caretaker at Cove Cottage. He loved the cottage, the cove, the lake, and rugged Sugarloaf Mountain at its back. She found him at the log cabin under the towering hemlocks. He listened patiently to her stories of Cove Cottage, of her Henry, and her return. As she bid him farewell, she reached into her pocket to give him her favorite book of poems by Lew Sarratt. Tobin held the slender volume in his hands as she walked away. It fell open to the marked pages Mary knew so well: "God, let me flower as I will . . ."

John Tobin knows many of the legends. He was caretaker in the early 1920s when stories of the Indian and the rich man's lovely daughter were still new. He later met the rich man's daughter when she returned to the side of her dying husband. He said at first there seemed to be nothing mysterious about the log cabin under the drooping hemlocks, except for the stories of the romance and the lonesome Indian.

One winter, Tobin's friend Tom Kelly became ill and dropped out of school. Kelly's father worried about the dark depressions that hounded the young man. He asked Tobin to take care of him for the winter, and the two moved into the cabin. Snows and freezing wind lashed across Lake Superior and beat upon the cabin door. They piled another log on the fire, and slept cozy warm.

Tobin recalled Kelly's phobia of fire. He fussed unnecessarily with the burning logs, always making sure the sparks were brushed back from the hearth's edge.

Friends joined them at the cabin. Once, as they walked along a wet trail, someone dropped a burned-out match. Kelly turned back suddenly and angrily ground the fireless match into the mud with his heel.

The dark overhanging branches of the twisted hemlocks seemed a natural place for ghost stories, and the friends spent hours trying to frighten one another out of their wits. They moved from stories to experimenting with Ouija boards.

One starless night, Tobin and his four friends decided to experiment with extrasensory perception. They chose Kelly to be "it." As he waited outside the cabin for them to plan, the three remembered his phobia of fire. Someone suggested having him move the lantern from the center of the table. Kelly always made certain it was set squarely in the middle. He refused to remain in the cabin if it was anywhere near the edge. They chuckled in boyish delight, and called Kelly in. As Kelly entered the room they concentrated on transmitting that thought to him. Kelly walked straight to the table without a moment's hesitation, and moved the lantern to the edge of the southeast corner! Tobin said he and friends stopped the game right there.

Before the winter was over, the friends delved once more into the mystic. While Kelly tended the fire, they pledged that, after death, they would each try to find their way back to Cove Cottage. Each promised that if he were the surviving member of the clan, he would return to the Cottage to receive a message from the beyond. Then they disbanded, each going his own way.

Tobin said he heard no ghostly figures moving in the dark, but he sensed a strange uneasy something that seemed to move through the fog gathered on the point and through the trees. If anyone heard a woman weeping, nobody talked about it.

Tobin left the cabin to work on the ore boats of Lake Superior. Kelly died. The rest forgot the pledges made around Kelly's fire.

The wind howled around the cabin. It tore at the wooden steps and the screen on the door. The log walls rotted. Winter snow and summer sun crept through the holes on the porch roof. New owners bought the property and occasionally visited the cove.

One day, a tall young man came hiking over the western

rim of the mountain. He spotted the cabin crumbling under the hemlocks and shook his head at the decay. He located the owner in Chicago. She refused to sell, but offered to let him use the cabin if he wanted to fix it up.

Stewart is not his real name; even now, he refuses to have his name linked with the cabin. Stewart hauled in boards and nails to make the cabin waterproof. On afternoon trips to the cove, the cabin seemed to welcome Stewart and his wife. They found the remnants of the red icehouse the Indian had tended at the turn-of-the-century. The pinion for tying up the boat was still secured in the boulders at the cove.

Then Stewart decided to spend the night. He banked the fire and watched the flickering flames as the sun ducked behind the tall forest. The curtain of night fell black. Then he heard a woman's sobbing and icy chills crept along his spine. He dashed to the door and threw it open wide. Flashing his light into the darkness, he searched the yard, the icehouse, and the trees. Nothing. The crying always seemed to be one flicker beyond his beam of light. The sobbing stopped sometime in the night. On other nights at the cabin, Stewart said he heard mumbling voices. They came intermittently with the crying. Sometimes they were silent for nights on end. Sometimes there were bloodcurdling screams.

On one visit to the cove, Stewart was accompanied by a friend, a Catholic priest. During the visit, one of the priest's parishioners died. The local undertaker found the priest at the cabin. While the priest gathered up his possessions, a scream pierced the air.

"The undertaker talks about it yet," Stewart said. "He said nothing could persuade him to stay there overnight."

Others who claim to have heard the screams said it was probably no more than a bobcat prowling the woods, and the noises had nothing to do with the legend of the cove. Finally, when Stewart's wife refused to go there again, he decided to solve the mystery once and for all. He loaded a backpack with a week's supplies and hiked over the mountain trail.

At the cabin, he probed the eaves for possible holes where

the wind might squeeze through to make the eerie sounds. He searched along the cove for cracks and crevices in the boulders that could produce the crying in the night. He looked into the waters of Lake Superior for the source of voices, and up the chimney for the mysterious sobbing screams.

Stewart searched for five days and found nothing. Daily, he noted everything in his diary, describing in detail his methodical searches. On the fifth night, he sat by lamplight watching the flames licking up the chimney. The sound of muffled footsteps came softly through the log walls, then with a solid tread seemed to walk across the back porch. Stewart leaped for the door and yanked it open. The porch, the night, was empty.

Then he heard the voices in the cove. He ran around the cabin; the voices were always one step ahead. Sudden fear squeezed his chest as he remembered that he had left the cabin door ajar. He turned and ran back inside. The cabin was empty. He quickly bolted the door. The voices finally faded into the night, and he again heard the crying woman. She cried until the dawn.

Stewart picked up his pen. With trembling fingers, he scribbled some last notes in his diary and tucked it carefully into the bottom of his pack. In the morning, he hiked back home with the pack fastened securely to his back. At home, he reached for his diary to note his time of arrival. He searched through the entire pack. He spilled the contents onto the floor. The diary was gone.

Stewart hiked back to the cabin. He checked the trail and searched the cabin, but found no sign of the notebook. "I left the cabin and never went back again," he said.

Shingles rotted once more. Log walls caved in. All traces of the red icehouse disappeared. Someone nailed up a stray board here and there, and used the structure as an occasional picnic shelter from sudden rain.

In the late 1970s, snow was banked eight feet deep around the cabin when some college students hiked in from across the hills. They stacked logs in the old fireplace and waited for the flames to dance along the hearth. They grew warm and tired, and threw their sleeping bags on the floor beside the fire.

Outside, the temperature rose to above freezing. The snow changed to light rain, adding more weight to the heavy snow deposited on the creaking roof. Three of the campers noted the sagging timbers and set up their tent outside. During the night, another student, worried about the sagging roof, joined them.

Light rain pelted the roof all night. Fog swirled along the cove and mingled with the smoke and glowing embers of the fire. The sun was making a feeble effort to climb over the mountain when the roof collapsed on the three sleeping young men. One escaped from a hole in the south side of the room. Another woke up under falling timbers and wet snow. The third never knew what happened to him.

Rescue teams fought their way through chest-deep snow to the scene. Fire from the embers had spread to the remaining timbers, eating them away until only the fireplace remained. Tobin heard about the fire, and remembered Kelly. He had never met Stewart, or heard his story. He thought about the vow made many years ago and the promise to return for possible signals from the others, now dead. But when he talks about the pact made at the cove, he shakes his head and looks away. "I'll never go back there," he says.

Years later, some folks said the strange crying was caused by winds from Lake Superior squeezing through the cove where the Indian once moored the rich man's boats. Some said the sound came from behind the spot where the cabin once stood. Those who have heard the crying in the night shake their heads and tremble. Only bare traces of the spot (called the 'Crying Cabin' in recent years) stand in the tall thimbleberry bushes beneath the dark spruce and hemlock trees west of Marquette.

Epilogue

Dixie Franklin says her first encounter with a ghost came through the introduction of cousin playmates as they played together in deep East Texas. The "ghost" was called "Old Tory." She was an unfortunate soul who, some said, lived some distance down the country road. Her hair was matted like Spanish moss, streaked with white, and hung in loose strands across her face. She dragged one foot in the sand, moaning, running and stumbling, intent on catching any child within her grasp.

Since Old Tory didn't respond to calls, one cousin always consented to be "it" to try to tease her out of her hiding place in the shadows. It did not work though and Dixie never actually saw Old Tory.

To this day, the cousins vow the ghost was real, that Old Tory did indeed prowl the shadowed road at twilight.

As for Dixie, she has kept so busy pursuing other people's ghosts that she has yet to encounter her own.